ESSENTIALS OF
COLLEGE
ENGLISH

3rd Edition

Mary Ellen Guffey
Professor of Business Emerita
Los Angeles Pierce College

Carolyn M. Seefer
Professor of Business
Diablo Valley College

CONSULTING EDITOR
Elizabeth T. Tice, Ph.D.
College of General & Professional Studies
University of Phoenix

THOMSON

SOUTH-WESTERN

Australia · Canada · Mexico · Singapore · Spain · United Kingdom · United States

THOMSON

SOUTH-WESTERN

Essentials of College English 3rd Edition

Mary Ellen Guffey and Carolyn M. Seefer

VP/Editorial Director:
Jack W. Calhoun

VP/Editor-in-Chief:
George Werthman

Sr. Acquisitions Editor:
Jennifer Codner

Developmental Editor:
Mary Draper

Sr. Marketing Manager:
Larry Qualls

Sr. Production Editor:
Deanna Quinn

Technology Project Editor:
Christine Wittmer

Media Editor:
Kelly Reid

Manufacturing Coordinator:
Diane Lohman

Production House:
WordCrafters Editorial Services

Compositor:
BookMasters, Inc.

Printer:
Quebecor World, Dubuque, IA

Sr. Design Project Manager:
Michelle Kunkler

Internal and Cover Design:
Tin Box Studio, Cincinnati, OH

Cover Illustration:
© Laura Tedeschi/Stock Illustration
Source

CONTENTS

PREFACE TO STUDENT

Dear Student:

The third edition of *Essentials of College English* was written to assist college students and business professionals in reviewing English grammar, punctuation, style, and usage. It contains comprehensive, up-to-date information and numerous reinforcement exercises designed to lead career-oriented adults to mastery of the concepts. This streamlined textbook has been configured to meet the needs of accelerated, nontraditional programs and busy working adults who need only a refresher.

Depending on your current skills, you can spend as much or as little time in each chapter as is necessary. In this completely revised edition, you'll find the following features:

- *Hotline Queries* (commonly asked language questions and answers)
- Marginal annotations, including *Spot the Blooper* and *Study Tips*
- Numerous examples containing up-to-date business concepts and references
- Reinforcement exercises and Unit Review exercises
- Answers to odd-numbered Reinforcement exercises
- Answers to Unit Reviews

When you finish reading and studying this book, we personally guarantee that your language skills will be much better than when you started. You will feel more confident as you communicate on the job, both orally and in writing. However, your mind is not a computer and can't record everything for instant recall. Like most professionals, you will occasionally need reference books to find answers. That's why you'll probably want to keep this book, along with a good dictionary and a reference manual, for review and use after you leave this class.

If you have any comments about this book or suggestions for improvement, please write to us. We wish you well in your studies.

Dr. Mary Ellen Guffey
Professor of Business Emerita
Los Angeles Pierce College
Woodland Hills, California
meguffey@west.net

Carolyn M. Seefer
Professor of Business
Diablo Valley College
Pleasant Hill, California
cseefer@dvc.edu

NOUNS

OBJECTIVES

When you have completed the material in this chapter, you will be able to do the following:

- Define the eight parts of speech.
- Understand how nouns function in sentences.
- Form the plurals of regular and irregular nouns.
- Spell challenging plural nouns ending in *y*, *f* or *fe,* and *o.*
- Form the plurals of compound nouns, numerals, letters, degrees, and abbreviations.
- Recognize and use correctly the plural form of foreign nouns, personal titles, selected special nouns, and single-letter abbreviations.

The ability to communicate effectively is one of the most important skills you can possess. Excellent communication skills will help you perform effectively in the workplace and will help you succeed in your career. In today's high-tech and global work environment, communication skills are more important than ever, and you can expect to be doing more communicating than ever before. Employees at all levels must be able to communicate effectively, both orally and in writing. You will be participating in meetings, writing reports, and sending many e-mail messages. Businesspeople who never expected to be doing much writing on the job find that the Internet forces everyone to exchange written messages. As a result, businesspeople are increasingly aware of their communication skills. Misspelled words, poor grammar, sloppy punctuation—all these faults stand out glaringly when printed. Not only are people writing more, but their messages travel farther. Messages are seen by larger audiences than ever before.

As a businessperson, you will want to feel confident about your oral and written communication skills. You can become a better communicator and feel more confident about your skills by reviewing basic grammar, mechanics, and usage principles. This textbook and this course will help you achieve your goals. Improving your language skills is the first step toward success in your education, your career, and your life.

THE EIGHT PARTS OF SPEECH

The first step to improving your communication skills is recognizing the eight parts of speech. Doing so will help you develop the working vocabulary necessary to discuss and study the language. You especially need to recognize the parts of speech in the context of sentences. That's because many words function in more than one role. Only by analyzing the sentence at hand can you see how a given word functions.

The eight parts of speech in the English language are as follows:

NOUNS:	Name persons, places, things, qualities, concepts, activities
PRONOUNS:	Take the place of nouns
VERBS:	Express an action, an occurrence, or a state of being
ADJECTIVES:	Describe or limit nouns and pronouns
ADVERBS:	Describe or limit verbs, adjectives, and other adverbs
PREPOSITIONS:	Join nouns and pronouns to other words in a sentence
CONJUNCTIONS:	Connect words or groups of words
INTERJECTIONS:	Express strong feelings

This textbook will focus on the most challenging concepts related to these eight parts of speech. Because nouns play such an important role in writing and speaking, we'll discuss this part of speech first.

AN INTRODUCTION TO NOUNS

Nouns are important words in our language. Sentences revolve around nouns since these words function both as subjects and as objects of verbs. Nouns name the following:

PERSONS:	supervisor, granddaughter, Mr. Takahashi, Sophia
PLACES:	home, university, Snake River, Nova Scotia
THINGS:	computer, report, dog, information
QUALITIES:	flexibility, initiative, patience, honesty
CONCEPTS:	freedom, happiness, aspiration, knowledge
ACTIVITIES:	surfing, management, studying, eating

Common and Proper Nouns

Common nouns name generalized persons, places, things, qualities, concepts, and activities. Common nouns are generally not capitalized. Proper nouns name specific persons, places, and things and should always be capitalized. Rules for capitalization are presented in Chapter 14.

COMMON NOUNS

document	dog	software
organization	businessperson	radio
photocopier	company	newspaper

PROPER NOUNS

Bill of Rights	Labrador retriever	Norton SystemWorks
United Nations	Michael Dell	Motorola cell phone
Xerox machine	Coca-Cola Company	*The Wall Street Journal*

STUDY TIP

In making surnames plural, never change the original spellings. Adding *s* or *es* is acceptable, but changing *Kennedy* to *Kennedies* changes the original spelling.

Note: Common nouns following proper nouns are not capitalized.

The principal emphasis of this chapter will be on forming and spelling plural nouns, an area of confusion for many business writers.

PLURALS OF REGULAR AND IRREGULAR NOUNS

Singular nouns name one person, place, or thing. Plural nouns name two or more. Be careful not to use apostrophes (') to form plural nouns. Reserve the apostrophe to show possession. (Chapter 2 discusses possessive nouns in detail.) Regular nouns are made plural by adding *s* or *es* to the end of the singular noun.

■ *Most regular nouns* form the plural with the addition of *s*.

river, rivers	advantage, advantages	password, passwords
trial, trials	decision, decisions	hyperlink, hyperlinks
Johnson, the Johnsons	Clark, the Clarks	Juan, Juans

Note: Most proper nouns (*Johnson, Juan*) become plural the same way that common nouns do.

■ *Regular nouns ending in* **s, x, z, ch,** *or* **sh** form the plural with the addition of *es*.

fax, faxes	waltz, waltzes	loss, losses
fox, foxes	virus, viruses	bush, bushes
Bush, the Bushes	Lopez, the Lopezes	Ross, Rosses

Note: Because of space restrictions most dictionaries do *not* show plurals of *regular* nouns. Thus, if you look up the plural of *ranch*, you probably will not find it. Dictionaries *do* show the plurals of nouns that might be confusing or difficult to spell.

■ *Irregular nouns* form the plural by changing the spelling of the word.

child, children	man, men	woman, women
mouse, mice	goose, geese	tooth, teeth

CHALLENGING NOUN PLURALS

Your ability to spell certain challenging nouns can be improved greatly by studying the following rules and examples.

■ *Common nouns ending in* **y** form the plural in two ways.

a. When the *y* is preceded by a vowel (*a, e, i, o, u*), the plural is formed with the addition of *s* only.

attorney, attorneys	essay, essays	play, plays
survey, surveys	valley, valleys	Murray, the Murrays

b. When the *y* is preceded by a consonant (all letters other than vowels), the plural is formed by changing the *y* to *ies*.

baby, babies	company, companies	copy, copies
laboratory, laboratories	policy, policies	specialty, specialties

Note: This rule does NOT apply to the plural forms of proper nouns: *Sally, Sallys; January, Januarys; Billy, Billys; Henry, the Henrys; Lowry, the Lowrys.*

■ *Nouns ending in* **f** *or* **fe** follow no standard rules in the formation of plurals. Study the examples shown here, and use a dictionary when in doubt. When two forms are shown, the preferred appears first.

ADD *s*	CHANGE TO *VES*	BOTH FORMS RECOGNIZED
brief, briefs	half, halves	calves, calfs
proof, proofs	knife, knives	dwarfs, dwarves
plaintiff, plaintiffs	leaf, leaves	wharves, wharfs
staff, staffs	shelf, shelves	scarves, scarfs
sheriff, sheriffs	wife, wives	
Wolf, the Wolfs	wolf, wolves	

■ **Nouns ending in o** may be made plural by adding *s* or *es*.

a. When the *o* is preceded by a vowel, the plural is formed by adding *s* only.

studio, studios ratio, ratios portfolio, portfolios

b. When the *o* is preceded by a consonant, the plural is formed by adding *s* or *es*. Study the following examples, and again use your dictionary whenever in doubt. When two forms are shown, the preferred one appears first.

ADD *s*	ADD *ES*	BOTH FORMS RECOGNIZED
photo, photos	echo, echoes	cargoes, cargos
typo, typos	embargo, embargoes	commandos, commandoes
logo, logos	hero, heroes	mosquitoes, mosquitos
memo, memos	potato, potatoes	tornadoes, tornados
auto, autos	tomato, tomatoes	volcanoes, volcanos
Angelo, Angelos	veto, vetoes	zeros, zeroes

c. Musical terms ending in *o* always form the plural with the addition of *s* only.

alto, altos banjo, banjos libretto, librettos

cello, cellos soprano, sopranos piano, pianos

■ **Compound nouns** may be written as single words, may be hyphenated, or may appear as two words.

a. When written as single words, compound nouns form the plural by appropriate changes in the final element.

bookshelf, bookshelves printout, printouts letterhead, letterheads

stockholder, stockholders photocopy, photocopies payroll, payrolls

b. When written in hyphenated or open form, compound nouns form the plural by appropriate changes in the principal noun.

accounts payable bills of lading attorneys-at-law

editors in chief leaves of absence vice-chancellors

mayors-elect brothers-in-law runners-up

c. If the compound noun has no principal noun at all, the final element is made plural.

cure-alls get-togethers go-betweens

hang-ups has-beens know-it-alls

follow-ups trade-offs walk-throughs

d. Some compound noun plurals have two recognized forms. In the following list, the preferred form is shown first.

> attorneys general, attorney generals
>
> cupfuls, cupsful; teaspoonfuls, teaspoonsful
>
> courts-martial, court-martials; notaries public, notary publics

■ ***Numerals, alphabet letters, isolated words, and degrees*** are made plural by adding *s, es,* or *'s.* The trend is to use the *'s* only when necessary for clarity.

a. Numerals and uppercase letters (with the exception of *A, I, M,* and *U*) require only *s* in plural formation.

1990s	all Bs and Cs	the three Rs
401Ks	W-2s and 1040s	7s and 8s

b. Isolated words used as nouns are made plural with the addition of *s* or *es,* as needed for pronunciation.

ands, ifs, or buts	dos and don'ts	pros and cons
yeses and noes	ups and downs	ins and outs
(*OR* yeses and nos)		

c. Degrees are made plural with the addition of *s* following the last period.

A.A.s	B.S.s	Ph.D.s
R.N.s	M.B.A.s	M.D.s

d. Isolated lowercase letters and the capital letters *A, I, M,* and *U* require *'s* for clarity.

M's	p's and q's	A's

■ ***Abbreviations*** are usually made plural by adding *s* to the singular form. Notice the placement of the *s* and periods in the following examples.

c.o.d., c.o.d.s	CEO, CEOs	RSVP, RSVPs
DVD, DVDs	mgr., mgrs.	No., Nos.
wk., wks.	yr., yrs.	CPA, CPAs

The singular and plural forms of abbreviations for units of measurement are, however, often identical.

> deg. (degree or degrees) in. (inch or inches)
>
> ft. (foot or feet) oz. (ounce or ounces)

Some units of measurement have two plural forms.

> lb. or lbs. yd. or yds. qt. or qts.

SPECIAL PLURAL FORMS

Selected nouns borrowed from foreign languages and other special nouns require your attention because their plural forms can be confusing.

■ ***Nouns borrowed from foreign languages*** may retain a foreign plural. A few, however, have an Americanized plural form, shown in parentheses below. Check your dictionary for the preferred form.

Singular	Plural
alumna (*feminine*)	alumnae (pronounced a-LUM-nee)
alumnus (*masculine*)	alumni (pronounced a-LUM-ni)
analysis	analyses
appendix	appendixes, appendices
bacterium	bacteria
basis	bases
cactus	cacti (or cactuses)
criterion	criteria (or criterions)
curriculum	curricula (or curriculums)
datum	data*
diagnosis	diagnoses
erratum	errata
formula	formulae (or formulas)
hors d'oeuvre	hors d'oeuvres
memorandum	memoranda (or memorandums)
millennium	millennia (or millenniums)
parenthesis	parentheses
phenomenon	phenomena
thesis	theses

*See discussion in the Hotline Queries.

■ **Personal titles** may have both formal and informal plural forms.

Singular	Formal Plurals	Informal Plurals
Miss	the Misses Kelly	the Miss Kellys
Mr.	Messrs.* Sanchez and Larson	Mr. Sanchez and Mr. Larson
Mrs.	Mmes.† Stokes and Aboud	Mrs. Stokes and Mrs. Aboud
Ms.	Mses.‡ Freeman and Moya	Ms. Freeman and Ms. Moya

*Pronounced MES-erz (abbreviation of Messieurs)
†Pronounced May-DAHM (abbreviation of Mesdames)
‡Pronounced MIZ-ez (Ms. is probably a blend of Miss and Mrs.)

■ **Special nouns,** many of which end in *s*, may normally be *only* singular *or* plural in meaning. Other special nouns may be considered *either* singular *or* plural in meaning.

Usually Singular	Usually Plural	May Be Singular or Plural
aeronautics	belongings	species
mathematics	clothes	deer
mumps	earnings	Chinese
economics	scissors	salmon
news	premises	headquarters
genetics	pants	series
billiards	goods	Vietnamese
dominos	thanks	fish
checkers	trousers	gross

■ **Single-letter abbreviations** may be made plural by doubling the letter.

pp. (pages)	See pp. 18–21. (That is, pages 18 through 21)
ff. (and following)	See pp. 18 ff. (That is, page 18 and following pages)

You are now ready to complete the reinforcement exercises.

Businesspeople are very concerned about appropriate English usage, grammar, and style. This concern is evident in the number and kinds of questions called in to grammar hotline services across the country. Among the callers are business supervisors, managers, executives, clerks, administrative assistants, and word processing specialists. Writers, teachers, librarians, students, and other community members also seek answers to language questions.

Selected questions and appropriate answers to them will be presented in the following chapters. In this way you, as a student of business English, will understand the kinds of everyday communication problems encountered in the work world. The original questions in our Hotline Queries came from the Los Angeles Pierce College Business English Hotline, which is no longer in service. More recently, questions have come from grammar hotline services across the country. You may download a list of grammar hotlines in the United States and Canada at the Tidewater Community College Writing Center Web site at **http://www.tcc.edu/students/ resources/writcent/GH/index.htm.**

Q: **We're having a big argument in our office. What's correct? *E-mail, e-mail, email,* or *Email?* And is it *on-line* or *online? Website, Web site, web site,* or *website?***

A: In the early days most people capitalized *E-mail* and hyphenated *on-line*. With increased use, however, both of these forms have been simplified: *e-mail* and *online,* which we recommend. Although the *Merriam-Webster College Dictionary,* Tenth edition (our standard reference) clings to *E-mail* when used as a noun, it does recognize the lowercase form for the verb form (*I will e-mail my response to you*). In our observation most publications today are moving toward *e-mail* for both noun and verb forms and *online* for both adjective and adverb functions. In regard to *Web site,* we recommend the capitalized, two-word form. Capitalizing *Web* is logical since it is a shortened form for World Wide Web, just as *Net* is a shortened form for the Internet. You might want to check with your company's in-house style manual for its preferred style for all of these words.

Q: **Could you help me spell the plurals of *do* and *don't?***

A: In forming the plurals of isolated words, the trend today is to add *s* and no apostrophe. Thus, we have *dos* and *don'ts.* Formerly, apostrophes were used to make isolated words plural. However, if no confusion results, make plurals by adding *s* only. Most readers will not confuse the lowercase *dos* for the acronym *DOS,* which stands for "disk operating system."

Q: **One member of our staff consistently corrects our use of the word *data* . He says the**

word is always plural. Is it never singular?

A: The word *data* is indeed plural; the singular form is *datum*. Through frequent usage, however, *data* has recently become a collective noun. Collective nouns may be singular or plural depending on whether they are considered as one unit or as separate units. For example, *These data are much different from those findings.* Or, *This data is conclusive.*

Q: What is the name of a group of initials that form a word? Is it an abbreviation?

A: A word formed from the initial letters of an expression is called an *acronym* (pronounced ACK-ro-nim). Examples: *scuba* from *self-contained underwater breathing apparatus,* and *RAM* from *random-access memory.* Acronyms are usually pronounced as a single word and are different from abbreviations. Expressions such as *FBI* and *dept.* are abbreviations, not acronyms. Notice that an abbreviation is pronounced letter by letter (*F, B, I*), whereas an acronym is pronounced as a word (*MADD,* which stands for *Mothers Against Drunk Driving*).

Q: In e-mail messages is it acceptable to use abbreviations such as IMHO (in my humble opinion), ROTFL (rolling on the floor laughing), LOL (laughing out loud), and TIA (thanks in advance)?

A: Among close friends who understand their meaning, such abbreviations are certainly acceptable. But in business messages, these abbreviations are too casual and too obscure. Many readers would have no idea what they mean. Smileys (or emoticons) such as :-) are also too casual for business and professional messages.

Q: Should an e-mail message begin with a salutation or some kind of greeting?

A: When e-mail messages are sent to company insiders, a salutation may be omitted. However, when e-mail messages travel to outsiders, omitting a salutation seems curt and unfriendly. Because the message is more like a letter, a salutation is appropriate (such as *Dear Courtney, Hi Courtney, Greetings,* or just *Courtney*). Including a salutation is also a visual cue to where the message begins. Some writers prefer to incorporate the name of the recipient in the first sentence (*Thanks, Courtney, for responding so quickly.*)

Q: As a sportswriter, I need to know the plural of *hole-in-one.*

A: Make the principal word plural, *holes-in-one.*

Q: What is the plural form of the computer *mouse?*

A: *Mice* refers to both computer devices and rodents. Example: *We ordered new mice for our office computers.*

2

POSSESSIVE NOUNS

When you have completed the material in this chapter, you will be able to do the following:

- Distinguish between possessive nouns and noun plurals.
- Follow five steps in using the apostrophe to show ownership.
- Use apostrophe construction for animate nouns.
- Distinguish between descriptive nouns and possessive nouns.
- Make compound nouns, combined ownership nouns, organization names, and abbreviations possessive.
- Understand incomplete possessives.
- Avoid awkward possessives.
- Make difficult proper nouns possessive.

In this chapter you will learn how to use the apostrophe to make nouns possessive.

SPOT THE BLOOPER

From an ad promoting subscriptions to *The Record-Searchlight* [Redding, California]: "The North State Welcome's You!"

SHOWING POSSESSION WITH APOSTROPHES

Possession occurs when one noun (or pronoun) possesses another. Notice in the following phrases how possessive nouns show ownership, origin, authorship, or measurement:

> Susan Nguyen's computer (ownership)
>
> Florida's citizens (origin)
>
> Michael Chabon's writings (authorship)
>
> three years' time (measurement)

SPOT THE BLOOPER

From Lois and Selma DeBakey's collection of bad medical writing: "The receptionist called the patients names." (How does the omitted apostrophe alter the meaning?)

In expressing possession, speakers and writers have a choice. They may show possession with an apostrophe construction, or they may use a prepositional phrase with no apostrophe:

> the computer of Susan Nguyen
>
> the citizens of Florida
>
> the writings of Michael Chabon
>
> the time of three years

The use of a prepositional phrase to show ownership is more formal and tends to emphasize the ownership word. The use of the apostrophe construction to show ownership is more efficient and more natural, especially in conversation. In writing, however, placing the apostrophe can be perplexing. Here are five simple but effective steps that will help you write possessives correctly.

Five Steps in Using the Apostrophe Correctly

1. **Look for possessive construction.** Usually two nouns appear together. The first noun shows ownership of (or a special relationship to) the second noun.

   the woman['s] briefcase
   the children['s] toys
   one month['s] wages
   several printers['] quotes
   the musicians['] instruments

2. **Reverse the nouns.** Use the second noun to begin a prepositional phrase. The object of the preposition is the ownership word.

   briefcase of the *woman*
   toys of the *children*
   wages of one *month*
   quotes of several *printers*
   instruments of the *musicians*

3. **Examine the ownership word.** To determine the correct placement of the apostrophe, you must know whether the ownership word ends in an *s* sound (such as *s, x,* or *z*).

4. **If the ownership word does not end in an *s* sound, add 's**.

   the woman's job
   the children's books
   a year's rent

5. **If the ownership word does end in an *s* sound, usually add only an apostrophe.**

   both investors' accounts
   musicians' instruments

If an extra syllable can be easily pronounced in the possessive form, add 's to singular nouns.

Singular Noun Ending in an *s* Sound; Extra Syllable Can Be Easily Pronounced	Add 's
station of the waitress[s]	waitress's station
desk of the boss[s]	boss's desk
den of the fox[s]	fox's den

A word of caution: Do NOT use apostrophes for nouns that simply show more than one of something (plural nouns). In the sentence *These companies are opening new branches in the West,* no apostrophes are required. The words *companies* and *branches* are plural; they are not possessive. In addition, be careful to avoid changing the spelling of singular nouns when making them possessive. For example, the *secretary's* desk (meaning one secretary) is NOT spelled *secretaries'.*

Pay particular attention to the following possessive constructions. The explanations and hints in parentheses will help you understand and remember these expressions.

a year's experience (the experience of one year)

ten years' experience (the experience of ten years)

a dollar's worth (the worth of one single dollar)

twenty dollars' worth (the worthy of twenty dollars)

your money's worth (the worth of your money)

today's newspaper (there can be only one today)

tomorrow's appointments (there can be only one tomorrow)

the stockholders' meeting (we usually assume that a meeting involves more than one person)

The guides for possessive construction presented thus far cover the majority of possessives found in business writing.

CHALLENGING POSSESSIVE CONSTRUCTIONS

You can greatly improve your skill in using apostrophes by understanding the following especially challenging possessive constructions.

■ *Animate versus inanimate nouns.* As a matter of style, some writers prefer to reserve the apostrophe construction for nouns that represent people, animals, and other living entities (such as trees or organizations). For inanimate nouns they use prepositional phrases or simple adjectives.

wing of the airplane, or airplane wing (better than *airplane's wing*)

color of the desk, or the desk color (better than *desk's color*)

terms of the contract, or contract terms (better than *contract's terms*)

STUDY TIP

To identify descriptive nouns, ask whether ownership is involved. Does *Department* belong to *Sales?* Is *industry* possessed by *electronics?* When the answer is no, omit the apostrophe.

■ *Descriptive versus possessive nouns.* When nouns provide description or identification only, the possessive form is NOT used. Writers have the most problems with descriptive nouns ending in *s,* such as *Claims* Department. No apostrophe is needed, just as none is necessary in *Legal* Department.

Sales Department (not *Sales' Department*)

the electronics industry (not *electronic's industry*)

Los Angeles Dodgers (not *Los Angeles' Dodgers*)

United States Army (not *United States' Army*)

■ *Compound nouns.* Make compound nouns possessive by adding an apostrophe or *'s* to the final element of the compound.

brother-in-law's birthday (singular)

editor in chief's office (singular)

attorneys-general's cases (plural)

stockholders' portfolios (plural)

■ *Incomplete possessives.* When the second noun in a possessive noun construction is unstated or implied, the first noun is still treated as possessive.

I left my umbrella at Colleen's [*house*].

They are meeting at the lawyer's [*office*] to discuss the testimony.

This year's sales are higher than last year's [*sales*].

■ *Separate or combined ownership.* When two nouns express separate ownership, make both nouns possessive. When two nouns express combined ownership, make only the *second* noun possessive.

SEPARATE OWNERSHIP	COMBINED OWNERSHIP
landlords' and tenants' rights	the husband and wife's business
Nadine's and Mike's cell phones	my aunt and uncle's home

■ *Names of organizations.* Organizations with possessives in their names may or may not use apostrophes. Always follow the style used by the individual organization. (Consult the organization's stationery, directory listing, or Web site if you're unsure.)

ORGANIZATION NAME CONTAINS APOSTROPHE	ORGANIZATION NAME DOES NOT CONTAIN APOSTROPHE
McDonald's	Starbucks
Noah's Bagels	Sears
Domino's Pizza	Marshalls
Kinko's	Mrs. Fields

■ *Abbreviations.* Make abbreviations possessive by following the same guidelines as for animate nouns.

AMA's annual convention	both CEOs' signatures
CNN's coverage	Marketing Dept.'s memo

■ *Awkward possessives.* When the addition of an apostrophe results in an awkward construction, show ownership by using a prepositional phrase.

AWKWARD:	my sister's attorney's advice
IMPROVED:	advice of my sister's attorney
AWKWARD:	my company's conference room's equipment
IMPROVED:	the equipment of my company's conference room
AWKWARD:	her boss, Mr. Wilde's, office
IMPROVED:	office of her boss, Mr. Wilde

MAKING DIFFICULT PROPER NOUNS POSSESSIVE

Of all possessive forms, individuals' names—especially those ending in *s* sounds—are the most puzzling to business communicators, and understandably so. Even experts don't always agree on the possessive form for singular proper nouns.

Traditionalists, as represented in *The Chicago Manual of Style (CMS)* and *The Modern Language Association (MLA) Style Manual,* prefer adding *'s* to singular proper nouns that end in *s* sounds to make them possessive. On the other hand, writers of more popular literature, as represented in *The Associated Press Stylebook and Libel Manual,* prefer the simpler style of adding just an apostrophe to singular proper nouns to make them possessive. You may apply either style, but be consistent. Please note in the following examples that the style choice applies *only* to singular names ending in *s* sounds. Plural names are always made possessive with the addition of an apostrophe only. Study the examples shown.

Singular Name	Singular Possessive— Traditional	Singular Possessive— Popular	Plural Possessive
Mr. Harris	Mr. Harris's	Mr. Harris'	the Harrises'
Ms. Sanchez	Ms. Sanchez's	Ms. Sanchez'	the Sanchezes'
Mr. Lewis	Mr. Lewis's	Mr. Lewis'	the Lewises'
Ms. Horowitz	Ms. Horowitz's	Ms. Horowitz'	the Horowitzes'

SUMMARY

Here's a summary of the possessive rule that should be easy to remember: If an ownership word does not end in an *s*, add *'s*. If the ownership word does end in an *s*, add just an apostrophe—unless you can easily pronounce an extra syllable. If you can pronounce that extra syllable, add *'s*.

You are now ready to complete the reinforcement exercises.

HOTLINE QUERIES

Q: Can you please explain something that is puzzling me? I thought that inanimate objects were not supposed to show possession. But how about the expression *a stone's throw?* A stone is certainly not alive!

A: Some common expressions are personified; that is, the nouns in these expressions are thought of as if they had human qualities. Here are a few examples: *at arm's length, for heaven's sake, in today's world,* and *a tone's throw.*

Q: In preparing an announcement for sales reps, our sales manager wrote about *a two months' training period.* I wanted to make it *a two-month training period.* Who is right?

A: Actually, you both are correct! The expression *two months' training period* is possessive (training period of two months).

If the expression is *two-month training period,* it is descriptive and no apostrophe is required. Only a slight difference in wording distinguishes a descriptive phrase from a possessive phrase. Sometimes it is hard to tell them apart.

Q: Where should the apostrophe go in *employee's handbook?* And what about *driver's license?*

A: This is tricky. If the writer considers the handbook from one employee's point of view, the expression is singular: *employee's handbook.* This is also true of expressions such as *driver's license* and *owner's manual.* If the writer is referring to a group, the references are plural: *employees' handbook* (a handbook for all employees), *drivers' licenses* (the licenses of all drivers), *owners' manuals* (the manuals of all owners). But you should also know that a few organizations prefer to use these terms as adjectives: *employee handbook, driver license, owner manual, employee handbook.*

Q: **I work for the Supreme Court in Arizona, and I have a problem with the following sentence:** *The plaintiff was in fact fired ostensibly for violating Denny's alcoholic beverage service policy.* **How do I make possessive a proper name that is already possessive?**

A: As you suspected, you can't add another apostrophe. In the interest of clarity, I would consider the name descriptive, thus avoiding an additional *'s.* You would write *Denny's alcoholic beverage service policy.* By the same reasoning, you would not add another apostrophe to anything possessed by *McDonald's.*

Q: **Why does** *Martha's Vineyard* **have an apostrophe while** *Harpers Ferry* **doesn't?**

A: The federal government maintains a Board on Geographic Names in the U.S. This board has a policy that "geographic names in the U.S. should not show ownership of a feature." British maps, says board secretary Roger Payne, are "littered with apostrophes." To avoid such clutter, the board allows no possessive on any federal maps or documents, unless previously dispensated. Only four geographic names have dispensations: Martha's Vineyard, (Massachusetts), Carlos Elmer's Joshua View (Arizona), Ike's Point (New Jersey), and John E.'s Pond (Rhode Island). You can find out more at **http://geonames.usgs. gov/bgn.html.**

Q: **I wonder if the possessive is correctly expressed in this sentence that I'm transcribing:** *I appreciate the candor of both you and Neil in our conversation.* **Shouldn't both** *you* **and** *Neil* **be made possessive?**

A: No. It would be very awkward to say *your and Neil's candor.* It's much better to use the *of* construction, thus avoiding the awkward double possessive.

Q: **Is there an apostrophe in** *Veterans Day,* **and if so, where does it go?**

A: *Veterans Day* has no apostrophe, but *New Year's Day* does have one.

Q: **As the holiday season approaches, I'm wondering whether it's** *Season's Greetings* **or** *Seasons' Greetings.*

A: If you are referring to one season, it's *Season's Greetings.*

PRONOUNS

OBJECTIVES

When you have completed the material in this chapter, you will be able to do the following:

- Understand basic uses of nominative-, objective-, and possessive-case pronouns.
- Choose the correct pronoun in compound constructions, comparatives, appositives, and reflexive constructions.
- Use *who/whoever, whom/whomever,* and *whose* appropriately.
- Make personal pronouns agree with their antecedents in number and gender.
- Understand the traditional use of common gender and be able to use its alternatives with sensitivity.
- Make personal pronouns agree with subjects joined by *or* or *nor,* indefinite pronouns, and collective nouns.

Pronouns are words that substitute for nouns and other pronouns. They enable us to speak and write without awkward repetition. Grammatically, pronouns may be divided into seven types (personal, relative, interrogative, demonstrative, indefinite, reflexive, and reciprocal). Rather than consider all seven pronoun types, this textbook will be concerned only with those pronouns that cause difficulty in use.

PERSONAL PRONOUNS

Personal pronouns indicate the person speaking, the person spoken to, or the person or object spoken of. Notice in the following table that personal pronouns change their form (or *case*) depending on who is speaking (called the *person*), how many are speaking (the *number*), and the sex (or *gender*) of the speaker. For example, the third-person feminine objective singular case is *her.* Most personal pronoun errors by speakers and writers involve faulty usage of case forms. Study this table to avoid errors in personal pronoun use.

STUDY TIP

This list is so important that you must memorize it. You must also know how these pronouns function in sentences.

	NOMINATIVE CASE*		OBJECTIVE CASE		POSSESSIVE CASE	
	SING.	PLURAL	SING.	PLURAL	SING.	PLURAL
FIRST PERSON (person speaking)	I	we	me	us	my, mine	our, ours
SECOND PERSON (person spoken to)	you	you	you	you	your, yours	your, yours

	NOMINATIVE CASE*		OBJECTIVE CASE		POSSESSIVE CASE	
	SING.	PLURAL	SING.	PLURAL	SING.	PLURAL
THIRD PERSON (person(s) or thing(s) spoken of)	he, she, it	they	him, her, it	them	his, her, hers, its	their, theirs

*Some authorities prefer the term *subjective case*.

Basic Use of the Nominative Case

Nominative-case pronouns are used primarily as the subjects of verbs. Every verb or verb phrase, regardless of its position in a sentence, has a subject. If that subject is a pronoun, it must be in the nominative case.

> *I* thought *she* would pay me back.
> *We* thought that *they* were using instant messaging.

Nominative-case pronouns also perform as subject complements. To understand what a *subject complement* is, you must know what a *linking verb* is. Verbs that express a state of being generally link to the subject words that describe or rename it. Some linking verbs are *am, is, are, was, were, be, being,* and *been.* Other linking verbs express the senses: *feels, appears, tastes, sounds, seems, looks.* A pronoun that follows a linking verb and renames the subject must be in the nominative case. (Linking verbs will be discussed in more detail in Chapter 4.)

> It *was I* who called the meeting.
> I'm sure it *is she* who usually picks up the office mail.
> If you *were I,* what would you do?

When a verb of several words appears in a phrase, look at the final word of the verb. If it is a linking verb, use a nominative pronoun.

> It *might have been they* who left the message.
> The driver *could have been he.*
> If the owner *had been I,* your money would have been refunded.

In conversation it is common to say, *It is me,* or more likely, *It's me.* Careful speakers and writers, though, normally use nominative-case pronouns after linking verbs. If the resulting constructions sound too "formal," revise your sentences appropriately. For example, instead of *It is I who placed the order,* use *I placed the order.* Remember, when answering the telephone, careful speakers will say, *This is she* or *This is he.* To sound natural, however, they will say, *This is . . .* and give their name.

Basic Use of the Objective Case

Objective-case pronouns most commonly are used in two ways.

■ *Object of a verb.* When pronouns act as direct or indirect objects of verbs, they must be in the objective case.

> The manager gave *them* a tour of the building.
> Ellen took *him* to the doctor.
> The receptionist led *me* back to the recruiter's office.

■ *Object of a preposition.* The objective case is used for pronouns that are objects of prepositions.

A letter signed by *us* was sent to *him.*
A package for *her* arrived at 10 a.m.
Just between *you* and *me,* the negotiations have stalled.

When the words *between, but, like,* and *except* are used as prepositions, errors in pronoun case are likely to occur. To avoid such errors, isolate the prepositional phrase, and then use an objective-case pronoun as the object of the preposition (*every employee [but Tom and him] completed the form*).

Basic Use of the Possessive Case

Possessive pronouns show ownership. Unlike possessive nouns, however, possessive pronouns require no apostrophes. Study the possessive pronouns in the following table. Notice the absence of apostrophes. Do not confuse possessive pronouns with contractions. Contractions are shortened (contracted) forms of subjects and verbs, such as *it's* (for *it is* or *it has*), *there's* (for *there is*), *they're* (for *they are*), and *you're* (for *you are*). In these examples the apostrophes indicate omitted letters.

POSSESSIVE PRONOUNS	CONTRACTIONS
Those seats are *theirs.*	*There's* not a seat left on the plane.
My iguana has escaped from *its* cage.	*It's* an unusual pet.
Your presentation will be fine.	*You're* the next speaker.

CHALLENGES IN USING PERSONAL PRONOUNS

Choosing the correct personal pronouns in compound constructions, comparatives, and appositives requires a good understanding of the following guidelines.

Compound Subjects and Objects

When a pronoun appears in combination with a noun or another pronoun, special attention must be given to case selection. Use this technique to help you choose the correct pronoun case: Ignore the extra noun or pronoun and its related conjunction, and consider separately the pronoun in question to determine what the case should be.

COMPOUND SUBJECTS:

[Allison and] *he* registered for the seminar. (Ignore *Allison and.*)
[You and] *I* must write the report. (Ignore *you and.*)

COMPOUND OBJECTS:

Jingfang asked [you and] *me* for help. (Ignore *you and.*)
Will you allow [Rasheed and] *them* to join you? (Ignore *Rasheed and.*)

Notice in the first sentence, for example, that when *Allison and* is removed, the pronoun *he* must be selected because it functions as the subject of the verb. In the third sentence when *you and* is removed, the pronoun *me* must be selected because it functions as the object of the verb.

Comparatives

In statements of comparison, words are often implied but not actually stated. To determine pronoun case in only partially complete comparative statements introduced by *than* or *as,* always mentally finish the comparative by adding the implied missing words.

> Shelley earns as much as *he.* (Shelley earns as much as *he* [not *him*] earns.)
> Nader Sharkes is a better cook than *she.* (. . . better cook than *she* [not *her*] is.)
> Does her attitude annoy you as much as *me?* (. . . as much as it annoys *me* [not *I*].)

Notice in the following examples how different pronouns can change the meanings of comparatives. Although both of these sentences are grammatically correct, they have two entirely different meanings.

> My husband loves money as much as I. (This means *My husband loves money as much as I love money.*)
> My husband loves money as much as me. (This means *My husband loves money as much as he loves me.*)

Appositives

Appositives explain or rename previously mentioned nouns or pronouns. A pronoun in apposition takes the same case as that of the noun or pronoun with which it is in apposition. In order to determine more easily what pronoun case to use for a pronoun in combination with an appositive, temporarily ignore the appositive.

> *We* [consumers] are protected by laws. (Ignore *consumers.*)
> The responsibility belongs to *us* [citizens]. (Ignore *citizens.*)

OTHER PRONOUNS THAT DESERVE ATTENTION

Certain groups of pronouns deserve special attention because they can trip up writers and speakers. In this section you'll learn to handle reflexive pronouns (such as *myself* and *himself*) and the dilemma of *who, whom,* and *whose.*

Reflexive Pronouns

Reflexive pronouns that end in *–self* or *–selves* emphasize or reflect on their antecedents (the nouns or pronouns previously mentioned).

> The president *himself* greeted each winner. (Emphasizes *president*)
> He installed the computer *himself.* (Reflects on *he*)
> We hope the matter will resolve *itself.* (Reflects on *matter*)
> I will take care of this problem *myself.* (Reflects on *I*)
> The employees *themselves* finalized the health care contract. (Emphasizes *employees*)

Errors result when reflexive pronouns are used instead of personal pronouns. If no previously mentioned noun or pronoun is stated in the same sentence, use a personal pronoun instead of a reflexive pronoun.

> Address your questions to your manager or *me.* (Not *myself* because *I* does not appear in the sentence.)
> Brenda and *I* wrote the proposal. (Not *myself* because *I* does not appear elsewhere in the sentence.)

Please note that *hisself* and *themself* are substandard and should always be avoided. The word *theirselves* does not exist.

The Challenge of *who/whoever* and *whom/whomever*

The use of *who/whoever* and *whom/whomever* presents a continuing dilemma for speakers and writers. In conversation the correct choice of *who/whoever* or *whom/whomever* is especially difficult because of the mental gymnastics necessary to locate subjects and objects. The following guidelines explain when to use *who/whoever* and *whom/whomever*.

In conversation, speakers may have difficulty analyzing a sentence quickly enough to use the correct *who/whom* form. In writing, however, an author has ample time to scrutinize a sentence and make a correct choice—if the author understands the traditional functions of *who* and *whom*.

Who (or *whoever*) is the nominative-case form. Like other nominative-case pronouns, *who* or *whoever* may function as the subject of a verb or as the subject complement of a noun following a linking verb. *Whom* (or *whomever*) is the objective-case form. It may function as the object of a verb or as the object of a preposition.*

> *Who* do you think will be elected? (*Who* is the subject of *will be elected*.)
> Susan wondered *who* my boss is. (*Who* is the complement of *boss*.)
> *Whom* should we choose? (*Whom* is the object of *should choose*.)
> Edmund is the one to *whom* I wrote. (*Whom* is the object of *to*.)

How to Choose Between *who/whoever* and *whom/whomever*

The choice between *who/whoever* and *whom/whomever* becomes easier if the sentence in question is approached according to the following procedure:

1. Isolate the *who/whom* clause.
2. Invert the clause, if necessary, to restore normal subject–verb–object order.
3. Reword the sentence to substitute the nominative pronoun *he* (*she* or *they*) for *who* or the objective pronoun *him* (*her* or *them*) for *whom*.
   a. If the sentence sounds correct with *he*, *who* (or *whoever*) is the correct pronoun.

   b. If the sentence sounds correct with *him*, *whom* (or *whomever*) is the correct pronoun.

Study the following sentences and notice how the choice of *who/whoever* or *whom/whomever* is made:

> Here are the records of those (who/whom) we have selected.
>
> ISOLATE: _____ we have selected
>
> INVERT: we have selected _____
>
> SUBSTITUTE: we have selected __him__
>
> EQUATE: we have selected __whom__
>
> COMPLETE: Here are the records of those *whom* we have selected.

Whom may also function as the subject or object of an infinitive. Since little confusion results from these constructions, they will not be discussed.

Do you know (who/whom) his doctor is?

ISOLATE: _____ his doctor is

INVERT: his doctor is _____ (or _____ is his doctor)

SUBSTITUTE: his doctor is ___he___ (or ___he___ is his doctor)

EQUATE: his doctor is ___who___ (or ___who___ is his doctor)

COMPLETE: Do you know *who* his doctor is?

In choosing *who* or *whom*, ignore parenthetical expressions such as *I hope, we think, I believe,* and *you know.*

Manuel is the applicant (who/whom) we believe is best qualified.

ISOLATE: _____ we believe is best qualified

IGNORE: _____ [we believe] is best qualified

SUBSTITUTE: ___he___ is best qualified

EQUATE: ___who___ is best qualified

COMPLETE: Manuel is the applicant *who* we believe is best qualified.

EXAMPLES:

Whom do you think we should call? (Invert: You think we should call him/*whom*.)

The person to *whom* we gave our evaluation was Roshanda. (Invert: We gave our evaluation to her/*whom*.)

Do you know *who* the plaintiff is? (Invert: The plaintiff is he/*who*.)

Whom would you like to include in the acknowledgments? (Invert: You would like to include him/*whom*.)

As we've discussed, *whoever* is nominative and can be replaced with *he* in a sentence. *Whomever* is objective and can be replaced with *him* in a sentence. The selection of the correct form is sometimes complicated when *whoever* or *whomever* appears in clauses. These clauses may act as objects of prepositions, objects of verbs, or subjects of verbs. Within the clauses, however, you must determine how *whoever* or *whomever* is functioning in order to choose the correct form. Study the following examples and explanations.

Offer the clothes to *whoever* needs them. (The clause *whoever needs them* is the object of the preposition *to*. Within the clause itself, *whoever* acts as the subject of *needs* and is therefore in the nominative case. You can replace with *he needs them*.)

A scholarship will be given to *whoever* has the qualifications. (The clause *whoever has the qualifications* is the object of the preposition *to*. Within the clause, *whoever* acts as the subject of *has* and is therefore in the nominative case. You can replace with *he has the qualifications*.)

We will accept the name of *whomever* they nominate. (The clause *whomever they nominate* is the object of the preposition *of*. Within the clause, *whomever* is the object of *they nominate* and is therefore in the objective case. You can replace with *they nominate him*.)

The Use of *whose*

The pronoun *whose* functions as a possessive pronoun. Like other possessive pronouns, *whose* has no apostrophe. Do not confuse it with the contraction *who's*, which means "who is" or "who has."

We haven't decided *whose* presentation was more persuasive.
Whose applications were submitted by the deadline?
Please let me know *who's* on call this evening.
Do you know *who's* scheduled to give the keynote address?

FUNDAMENTALS OF PRONOUN–ANTECEDENT AGREEMENT

Pronouns enable us to communicate efficiently. They provide short forms that save us from the boredom of repetitive nouns. But they can also get us in trouble if the nouns to which they refer—their *antecedents*—are unclear. This section shows you how to avoid pronoun–antecedent problems. It also presents solutions to a major problem for sensitive communicators today—how to handle the *his/her* dilemma.

When pronouns substitute for nouns, the pronouns must agree with their antecedents in number (either singular or plural) and gender (masculine, feminine, or neuter). Here are suggestions for using pronouns effectively.

Making Pronoun References Clear

Do not use a pronoun if your listener or reader might not be able to identify the noun it represents.

UNCLEAR:	Ms. Harrison heard Luke tell Jason that *he* would be late.
CLEAR:	Ms. Harrison heard Luke tell Jason that Luke would be late.
UNCLEAR:	In the computer lab *they* do not allow you to eat.
CLEAR:	The lab supervisor does not allow anyone to eat in the computer lab.
	Or: Eating is not allowed in the computer lab.
UNCLEAR:	When Dave Evola followed Brad Eckhardt as president, many of *his* policies were reversed.
CLEAR:	When Dave Evola followed Brad Eckhardt as president, many of Eckhardt's policies were reversed.

Making Pronouns Agree With Their Antecedents in Number

Pronouns must agree in number with the nouns they represent. If a pronoun replaces a singular noun, that pronoun must be singular. If a pronoun replaces a plural noun, that pronoun must be plural

Michelangelo felt that *he* was a failure. (Singular antecedent and pronoun)
Great *artists* often doubt *their* success. (Plural antecedent and pronoun)

If a pronoun refers to two nouns joined by *and,* the pronoun must be plural.

The *president* and the *stockholders* discussed *their* differences. (Plural antecedent and pronoun)
Mitchell and *Nancy* asked that suggestions be sent to *them*. (Plural antecedent and pronoun)

Pronoun–antecedent agreement can be complicated when words or phrases come between the pronoun and the word to which it refers. Disregard phrases such as those introduced by *as well as, in addition to,* and *together with*. Find the true antecedent and make the pronoun agree with it.

The *CEO*, together with her executive committee, is considering *her* strategy carefully. (Singular antecedent and pronoun)

The *department heads,* along with the CEO, have submitted *their* plans. (Plural antecedent and pronoun)

A female *member* of the group of protesting employees demanded that *she* be treated equally. (Singular antecedent and pronoun)

Company and organization names are generally considered singular. Unless the actions of the organization are attributed to individual representatives of that organization, pronouns referring to organizations should be singular.

Banana Republic is having *its* annual half-price sale.

Doctors Without Borders, in addition to other organizations, is expanding *its* efforts to provide emergency aid to victims of natural disasters.

Smith, Felker & Torres, Inc., plans to open *its* new branch in Chicago this year.

Making Pronouns Agree with Their Antecedents in Gender

Pronouns exhibit one of three *genders:* masculine (male), feminine (female), or neuter (neither masculine nor feminine). Pronouns must agree with their antecedents in gender.

Natalie ate *her* lunch. (Feminine gender)

Jeremy submitted *his* résumé. (Masculine gender)

The idea had *its* limits. (Neuter gender)

Choosing Alternatives to Common-Gender Antecedents

Occasionally, writers and speakers face a problem in choosing pronouns of appropriate gender. English has no all-purpose singular pronoun to represent indefinite nouns (such as *a student* or *an employee*). For this reason writers and speakers have, over the years, used masculine, or common-gender, pronouns to refer to singular nouns that might be either masculine or feminine. For example, in the sentence *An employee has his rights,* the pronoun *his* referred to its antecedent *employee,* which might name either a feminine or masculine person.

Communicators today, however, avoid masculine pronouns (*he, his*) when referring to indefinite singular nouns that could be masculine or feminine. Critics call these pronouns "sexist" because they exclude women. To solve the problem, sensitive communicators rewrite sentences requiring such pronouns. Although many alternatives exist, here are three common options:

COMMON GENDER:	*A passenger* must show *his* passport before boarding.
ALTERNATIVE NO. 1:	*Passengers* must show *their* passports before boarding.
ALTERNATIVE NO. 2:	*A passenger* must show *a* passport before boarding.
ALTERNATIVE NO. 3:	*A passenger* must show *his or her* passport before boarding.
WRONG:	*A passenger* must show *their* passports before boarding.

In Alternative No. 1 the subject has been made plural to avoid the need for a singular common-gender pronoun. In Alternative No. 2 the pronoun is omitted, and an article is substituted, although at the cost of making the original meaning less emphatic. In Alternative No. 3 both masculine and feminine references (*his or her*) are used. Because the latter construction is wordy and clumsy, frequent use of it should be avoided. Substituting the plural pronoun *their* is incorrect since it does not agree with its singular antecedent, *passenger.*

SPECIAL PRONOUN–ANTECEDENT CHALLENGES

The following guidelines will help you avoid errors in pronoun-antecedent agreement in special cases. These special instances include sentences in which the antecedents (a) are joined by *or* or *nor*, (b) are indefinite pronouns, or (c) are collective nouns.

Antecedents Joined by *or* or *nor*

When antecedents are joined by *or* or *nor*, the pronoun should agree with the antecedent closer to it.

> Either Sondra or *Janine* left *her* briefcase in the conference room.
> Neither the employees nor the *supervisor* expect to see *his* salary increased this year.
> Neither the supervisor nor the *employees* expect to see *their* salaries increased this year. (Notice that *salaries* must also be made plural.)

You may be wondering why antecedents joined by *and* are treated differently from antecedents joined by *or* or *nor*. The conjunction *and* joins one plus one to make two antecedents; hence a plural pronoun is used. The conjunctions *or* and *nor* require a choice between two antecedents. Always match the pronoun to the closer antecedent.

Indefinite Pronouns as Antecedents

Pronouns such as *anyone, something,* and *anybody* are called *indefinite* because they refer to no specific person or object. Some indefinite pronouns are always singular; others are always plural.

Always Singular		Always Plural
anybody	everything	both
anyone	neither	few
anything	nobody	many
each	no one	several
either	nothing	
everybody	somebody	
everyone	someone	

When indefinite pronouns function as antecedents of pronouns, make certain that the pronoun agrees with its antecedent. Do not let prepositional phrases obscure the true antecedent.

> *Someone* in the men's league left *his* car lights on.
>
> *Each* of the corporations has *its* own home office.
>
> *Few* of our employees have *their* own private parking *spaces.* (Notice that *spaces* is also plural.)
>
> *Several* of our branches list *their* job openings on the company's intranet.

The words *either* and *neither* can be confusing. When these words stand alone and function as pronoun subjects, they are always considered singular.

> *Either* of the women *is* able to see *her* personnel record. (*Either* is a singular pronoun and functions as the subject of the sentence. It controls the singular verb *is*. *Either* is also the antecedent of the pronoun *her.*)

STUDY TIP

When *either* or *neither* is followed by an *of* phrase, it's functioning as a singular pronoun. For example, *Either of the books is available.*

You should note that *each, every,* and *many a* often function as adjectives. If the limiting adjectives *each, every,* and *many a* describe either noun or both nouns in a compound antecedent, that antecedent is considered singular.

> *Each* player and coach on the women's soccer team has *her* assigned duties.
> *Many a* son and father will receive *his* award at the banquet.
> *Every* reference, citation, and notation *is* checked for accuracy.

Collective Nouns as Antecedents

Words such as *jury, faculty, committee, staff, union, team, flock,* and *group* are called *collective* nouns because they refer to a collection of people, animals, or objects. Such words may be either singular or plural depending on the mode of operation of the collection to which they refer. When a collective noun operates as a unit, it is singular. When the elements of a collective noun operate separately, the collective noun is plural.

> No action can be taken until the *committee* announces *its* decision. (*Committee* operating as one unit)
> The *jury* rendered *its* verdict. (*Jury* operating as one unit)
> The *jury* took *their* seats in the courtroom. (*Jury* operating as individuals)

However, if a collective noun is to be used in a plural sense, the sentence can often be made to sound less awkward by the addition of a plural noun (*The jury members took their seats in the courtroom*).

You are now ready to complete the reinforcement exercises.

HOTLINE QUERIES

Q: On the radio I recently heard a talk-show host say, *My producer and myself . . . .* A little later that same host said, *Send any inquiries to the station or myself at this address.* This sounded half right and half wrong, but I would have trouble explaining the problem. Can you help?

A: The problem is a common one: use of a reflexive pronoun (*myself*) when it has no preceding noun on which to reflect. Correction: *My producer and I* and *Send inquiries to the station or me.* Reflexive pronouns like *myself* should be used only with obvious antecedents, such as *I, myself, will take the calls.* Individuals in the media often misuse reflexive pronouns, perhaps to avoid sounding egocentric with overuse of *I* and *me.*

Q: In an article in *U.S. News & World Report* about the U.S. Embassy's proposal to purchase new dishware, I saw this sentence: *The location of the crest on the teacups and demitasse cups shall be centered so that when held with the right hand, the crest can be seen by* _whomever_ *is sitting directly in front of the person holding the cup.* Is this correct?

A: Hey, you've found a bona fide blooper! Many writers think that an objective-case pronoun MUST follow the preposition *by.* In this case, however, an entire clause follows the preposition. Within that clause *whoever* functions as the subject. Good detective work! *Whomever* should be *whoever.* You can replace the clause with *he is sitting directly in front of . . . .*

Q: Here's a sentence we need help with: *We plan to present the contract to whoever makes the lowest bid.* My supervisor recommends *whoever* and I suggest *whomever.* Which of us is right?

A: Your supervisor. The preposition *to* has as its object the entire clause (*whoever makes the lowest bid*). Within that clause *whoever* functions as the subject of the verb *makes;* therefore, the nominative-case form *whoever* should be used.

Q: I'm disgusted and infuriated at a New York University advertisement I just saw in our newspaper. It says, *It's not just* _who_ *you know . . . .* Why would a leading institution of learning use such poor grammar?

A: Because it sounds familiar. But familiarity doesn't make it correct. You're right in recognizing that the proper form is *whom* (isolate the clause *you know him* or *whom*). The complete adage—or more appropriately, cliché—correctly stated is: *It's not what you know but* _whom_ *you know.*

Q: I often catch myself using the response *me too* when I agree or have taken part in the same activity as someone else. For example, a friend will say, *I loved the new Tom Hanks film,* and I'll respond, *Me too.* Is this a correct use of the pronoun *me?*

A: Although you'll hear this response commonly used, grammatically it's incorrect. When you respond with these words, you're really saying, *Me loved the new Tom Hanks film too.* However, responding with *I too,* which is grammatically correct, would probably sound too stuffy. If you want to respond correctly but naturally, try saying something like *So did I* or *I did too.*

Q: Is it correct to say *Brad and myself were chosen . . . ?*

A: No. Use the nominative-case pronoun *I* instead of *myself.*

HOTLINE QUERIES

Q: Tell me it's not true! I just heard that the word *doh,* which is uttered frequently by the Homer Simpson character, was recently added to the *Oxford English Dictionary.* Surely this is an urban legend.

A: It's true. The word *doh* was added to the *Oxford English Dictionary,* long considered the foremost authority on the English Language, in June 2001. Its editors decided that the word *doh* is so universally accepted and recognized that it warranted formal recognition. This certainly proves what an effect popular culture has on our language. However, keep in mind that just because a word appears in the dictionary doesn't mean that it's appropriate for business communicators to use.

Q: Is *every day* one word or two in this case? *We encounter these problems every day.*

A: In your sentence it is two words. When it means "ordinary," it is one word (*she wore everyday clothes*). If you can insert the word *single* between *every* and *day* without altering your meaning, you should be using two words, as in your sentence.

Q: If I have no interest in something, am I *disinterested?*

A: No. If you lack interest, you are *uninterested.* The word *disinterested* means "unbiased" or "impartial" (*the judge was disinterested in the cases before him*).

Q: A fellow worker insists on saying, *I could care less.* Seems to me that it should be *I couldn't care less.* Who is right?

A: You are right. The phrase *I couldn't care less* has been in the language a long time. It means, of course, "I have little concern about the matter." Recently, though, people have begun to use *I could care less* with the same meaning. Most careful listeners realize that the latter phrase says just the opposite of its intent. Although both phrases are clichés, stick with *I couldn't care less* if you want to be clear.

VERBS: FUNDAMENTALS, VOICES, TENSES, AND PARTS

OBJECTIVES

When you have completed the material in this chapter, you will be able to do the following:

- Distinguish between action verbs and linking verbs.
- Recognize active- and passive-voice verbs.
- Use correctly verbs in the present, past, and future tenses.
- Understand the role of helping verbs.
- Recognize and use present and past participles appropriately.
- Use correctly over 60 irregular verbs.

Verbs are words that energize sentences. They tell what is happening, what happened, and what will happen. The verb is the most complex part of speech. A complete treatment of its forms and uses would require at least a volume. Our discussion of verbs will be limited to practical applications for businesspeople. In this chapter you'll learn about verb fundamentals including action and linking verbs, verb voices, and tenses. You'll also study helping verbs, present and past participles, and irregular verbs.

VERB FUNDAMENTALS

Verbs express an action, an occurrence, or a state of being.

> Alexandra <u>wrote</u> an excellent proposal. (Action)
> The winter holidays <u>end</u> the fall term. (Occurrence)
> Joe <u>is</u> the new technical writer. (State of being)

In relation to subjects (nouns or pronouns), verbs generally tell what the subject is doing or what is being done to the subject. Verbs may also link to the subject words that describe the subject or identify it. All sentences have at least one verb; many sentences will have more than one verb. Verbs may appear singly or in phrases.

> Stacy <u>submitted</u> her application to become a management trainee. (Action verb)
> Her résumé <u>is</u> just one page long. (Linking verb)
> She <u>has been training</u> to become a manager. (Verb phrase)
> Stacy <u>feels</u> bad that she <u>will be leaving</u> her old friends. (Linking verb and verb phrase)

Verbs may be classified into two broad categories: action verbs and linking verbs. Knowing how each category functions will help you use verbs correctly.

Action Verbs

Action verbs show the physical or mental action of a sentence. Examples of action verbs include *runs, studies, works, thinks,* and *dreams.* Some action verbs have *objects,* which can be nouns or pronouns.

> <u>Customers</u> <u>bought</u> <u>products</u>.
> Yesterday the <u>president</u> <u>called</u> <u>her</u>.
> <u>Krispy Kreme</u> <u>sells</u> <u>doughnuts</u> by the millions.

Objects usually answer the questions *what?* or *whom?* In the first example, the customers bought *what?* The object is *products.* In the second example, the president called *whom?* The object is *her.* In the third example, Krispy Kreme sells what? The object is *doughnuts.*

Not all action verbs require objects, as the following sentences illustrate.

> <u>Tran Phuong</u> <u>worked</u> in our Human Resources Department last summer.
> <u>Francesca</u> <u>listened</u> carefully to the lecture.
> <u>Stan</u> <u>dreams</u> of owning his own business one day.

Notice that the verbs in these sentences do not express actions directed toward persons or things. Prepositional phrases (*in our Human Resources Department, to the lecture, of owning*) and adverbs (*carefully*) do not receive the action expressed by the verbs. Prepositional phrases and adverbs do not function as objects of verbs.

Linking Verbs

Verbs that express a state of being generally link to the subject words that describe or rename it. Examples of linking verbs are *am, is, are, was, were, be, being,* and *been.* Other linking verbs express the senses: *feels, appears, tastes, sounds, seems, looks.* A noun, pronoun, or adjective that renames or describes the subject is called a *complement* because it *completes* the meaning of the subject.

> Angie <u>is</u> the <u>manager</u>. (*Manager* is a noun complement that completes the meaning of the sentence by renaming *Angie.*)
> Her salary <u>is</u> <u>excellent</u>. (*Excellent* is an adjective complement that completes the meaning of *salary.*)
> The caller <u>was</u> <u>he</u>. (*He* is a pronoun complement that completes the meaning of *caller.*)

Notice in the preceding sentences that the noun, pronoun, or adjective complements following these linking verbs do not receive action from the verb; instead, the complements *complete* the meaning of the subject.

VERB VOICES

Action verbs that have objects can fall into two categories depending on the receiver of the action of the verbs.

Active Voice

When the verb expresses an action directed by the subject toward the object of the verb, the verb is said to be in the *active voice.*

> <u>Stephanie</u> <u>answered</u> the telephone. (Action directed to the object, *telephone*)

Verbs in the active voice are direct and forceful; they clearly identify the doer of the action. For these reasons, writing that frequently uses the active voice is

SPOT THE BLOOPER

Advice in Harvard Medical School's *Heart Letter:* "Do not feel too badly about missing dosages of your pills."

vigorous and effective. Writers of business communications strive to use the active voice; in fact, it is called the *voice of business*.

In the passive voice, verbs always require a *helper*, such as *is, are, was, were, being,* or *been.*

A clue to passive voice is a prepositional phrase beginning with *by.*

Passive Voice

When the action in a verb is directed toward the subject, the verb is said to be in the *passive voice*. Study the following pairs:

PASSIVE:	The <u>figures</u> <u>are</u> <u>totaled</u> daily.
ACTIVE:	<u>We</u> <u>total</u> the figures daily.
PASSIVE:	The <u>lottery</u> <u>was</u> <u>won</u> by Jocelyn Iannucci.
ACTIVE:	<u>Jocelyn</u> <u>Iannucci</u> <u>won</u> the lottery.
PASSIVE:	Three <u>errors</u> <u>were</u> <u>made</u> in the report.
ACTIVE:	The <u>accountant</u> <u>made</u> three errors in the report.

Because the passive voice can be used to avoid mentioning the performer of the action, the passive voice is sometimes called the *voice of tact*. Notice how much more tactful the passive version of the last example in the previous list is. Although directness in business writing is generally preferable, in certain instances the passive voice is used when indirectness is desired.

VERB TENSES

English verbs change form (inflection) to indicate number (singular or plural), person (first, second, or third), voice (active or passive), and tense (time). To indicate precise time, English employs verb tenses. These tenses are used to indicate the present, the past, and the future.

Present Tense

Verbs in the present tense express current or habitual action. Present tense verbs may also be used in constructions showing future action.

We *order* office supplies every month. (Current or habitual action)
He *flies* to Indianapolis tomorrow. (Future action)

On a job applicant's cover letter: "I had strong interpersonal and communication skills."

Past Tense

Verbs in the past tense show action that has been completed. Regular verbs form the past tense with the addition of *d* or *ed*.

The Internal Revenue Service *needed* the forms yesterday.
The report *focused* on changes in our department.

Future Tense

Verbs in the future tense show actions that are expected to occur at a later time. Traditionally, the helper verbs *shall* and *will* have been joined with principal verbs to express future tense. In business writing today, however, the verb *will* is generally used as the helper to express future tense.

Daniel *will need* extra time to complete his next assignment.
You *will receive* the signed contract by August 31.

Summary of Verb Tenses

The following table summarizes the various forms employed to express the verb tenses:

	PRESENT TENSE		PAST TENSE		FUTURE TENSE	
	SING.	PLURAL	SING.	PLURAL	SING.	PLURAL
FIRST PERSON:	I need	we need	I needed	we needed	I will need	we will need
SECOND PERSON:	you need	you need	you needed	you needed	you will need	you will need
THIRD PERSON:	he, she, it needs	they need	he, she, it needed	they needed	he, she, it will need	they will need

Note that third-person singular verbs require an -s ending (*he needs*).

Be sure to use a dictionary to verify the spelling of verbs that change form. One must be particularly careful in spelling verbs ending in *y* (*hurry, hurries, hurried*) and verbs for which the final consonant is doubled (*occurred, expelled*).

Helping (Auxiliary) Verbs

A verb that combines with a main verb to convey information about tense, mood, or voice functions as a helping or auxiliary verb. The most common helping verbs are forms of *be (am, is, are, was, were, being, been),* forms of *do (does, did),* and forms of *have (has, had).* Other helping verbs include *may, must, ought, can, might, could, should, would, shall,* and *will.* As you will recall, the verb *be* and all its forms also function as linking verbs.

> Our manager *is* a funny guy. (The linking verb *is* joins the complement *guy* to the subject.)
> Our manager *is using* his computer. (The helping verb *is* combines with the main verb *using* to form a verb phrase whose object is *computer.*)

Whether functioning as a linking verb or as a helping verb, the verb *be* should be used in standard forms.

> Erin *is looking* for a new job. (Not *be looking*)
> She *is* lucky to have a computer. (Not *be*)

PRESENT AND PAST PARTICIPLES

To be able to use all the tenses of verbs correctly, you must understand the four principal parts of verbs: present, past, present participle, and past participle. You have already studied the present and past forms. Now, let's consider the participles.

Present Participle

The present participle of a regular verb is formed by adding *ing* to the present tense of the verb. When used in a sentence as part of a verb phrase, the present participle is preceded by a helping verb, such as *am, is, are, was, were, be,* and *been*.

> I *am printing* the proposal.
> You *are wasting* good paper.

Past Participle

The past participle of a regular verb is usually formed by adding a *d* or *ed* to the present tense of the verb. Like present participles, past participles must combine with one or more helping verbs (such as *has* or *have*).

Chandra *has checked* her data carefully.
Her data *has been checked* by Chandra.
We *should have finished* the project earlier.
The project *should have been finished* earlier.

IRREGULAR VERBS

Up to this point, we have considered only regular verbs. Regular verbs form the past tense by the addition of *d* or *ed* to the present tense form. Many verbs, however, form the past tense and the past participle irregularly. (More specifically, irregular verbs form the past tense by a variation in the root vowel and, commonly, the past participle by the addition of *en*.) A list of the more frequently used irregular verbs follows. Learn the forms of these verbs by practicing in patterns such as:

PRESENT TENSE: Today I ___**drive**___.

PAST TENSE: Yesterday I ___**drove**___.

PAST PARTICIPLE: In the past I have ___**driven**___.

Also note that irregular verbs form the present participle in the same way as regular verbs: by adding *ing* and a helper. Therefore, the present participle of *drive* is *driving*.

Frequently Used Irregular Verbs

PRESENT	PAST	PAST PARTICIPLE
arise	arose	arisen
be (am, is, are)	was, were	been
bear (to carry)	bore	borne
become	became	become
begin	began	begun
bite	bit	bitten
blow	blew	blown
break	broke	broken
bring	brought	brought
build	built	built
burst	burst	burst
buy	bought	bought
choose	chose	chosen
come	came	come
dig	dug	dug
do	did	done
draw	drew	drawn
drink	drank	drunk
drive	drove	driven
eat	ate	eaten
fall	fell	fallen
fight	fought	fought
fly	flew	flown
forbid	forbade	forbidden

PRESENT	PAST	PAST PARTICIPLE
forget	forgot	forgotten *or* forgot
forgive	forgave	forgiven
freeze	froze	frozen
get	got	gotten *or* got
give	gave	given
go	went	gone
grow	grew	grown
hang (to suspend)	hung	hung
hang (to execute)	hanged	hanged
hide	hid	hidden *or* hid
know	knew	known
lay (to place)	laid	laid
lead	led	led
leave	left	left
lend	lent	lent
lie (to rest)	lay	lain
lie (to tell a falsehood)	lied	lied
lose	lost	lost
make	made	made
pay	paid	paid
prove	proved	proved *or* proven
raise (to lift)	raised	raised
ride	rode	ridden
ring	rang	rung
rise (to move up)	rose	risen
run	ran	run
see	saw	seen
set (to place)	set	set
shake	shook	shaken
shrink	shrank	shrunk
sing	sang	sung
sink	sank	sunk
sit (to rest)	sat	sat
speak	spoke	spoken
spring	sprang	sprung
steal	stole	stolen
strike	struck	struck *or* stricken
swear	swore	sworn
swim	swam	swum
take	took	taken
tear	tore	torn
throw	threw	thrown
wake	woke	woken
wear	wore	worn
write	wrote	written

THREE PAIRS OF COMMONLY MISUSED IRREGULAR VERBS

The key to the correct use of the following pairs of irregular verbs lies in developing the ability to recognize the tense forms of each and to determine whether the verb needs a direct object.

Lie–Lay

These two verbs are confusing because the past tense of *lie* is spelled in exactly the same way that the present tense of *lay* is spelled. To be safe, you'll want to memorize these verb forms:

	PRESENT	PRESENT PARTICIPLE	PAST	PAST PARTICIPLES
NO OBJECT:	lie (to rest)	lying	lay	lain
REQUIRES OBJECT:	lay (to place)	laying	laid (not *layed*)	laid

The verb *lie* requires no direct object to complete its meaning.

> I *lie* down for a nap every afternoon. (Present tense. Note that *down* is not a direct object.)
> "*Lie* down," he told his dog. (Commands are given in the present tense.)
> The contract *is lying* on the desk. (Present participle)
> Yesterday I *lay* down for a nap. (Past tense)
> It *has lain* there for some time. (Past participle)

The verb *lay* must have a direct object to complete its meaning. The objects in the following sentences have been underlined.

> *Lay* the <u>report</u> over there. (Command in the present tense)
> The contractor *is laying* new <u>tile</u> in the entryway. (Present participle)
> He *laid* the <u>handouts</u> on the conference table. (Past tense)
> He *has laid* <u>bricks</u> all his life. (Past participle)

Sit–Set

Less troublesome than *lie–lay,* the combination of *sit–set* is nevertheless perplexing because the sound of the verbs is similar. The verb *sit* (past tense, *sat;* past participle, *sat*) means "to rest" and requires no direct object.

> Do you *sit* here often? (Present tense; *here* is not an object.)
> *Are* you usually *sitting* here in the morning? (Present participle)
> They *sat* in the theater through the closing credits. (Past tense)
> They *had sat* in the waiting room for two hours before they decided to leave. (Past participle)

The verb *set* (past tense, *set;* past participle, *set*) means "to place" and must have a direct object. The objects in the following sentences have been underlined.

> Letty usually *sets* her coffee <u>mug</u> there. (Present tense)
> She *is setting* her coffee <u>mug</u> here today. (Present participle)
> We *set* a <u>vase</u> of flowers on the receptionist's desk. (Past tense)
> We *had set* the <u>table</u> long before the guest arrived. (Past participle)

Rise–Raise

The verb *rise* (past tense, *rose;* past participle, *risen*) means "to go up" or "to ascend" and requires no direct object.

> The sun *rises* every morning in the east. (Present tense. *Every morning* is an adverbial phrase, not an object.)
> Our elevator *is rising* to the eleventh floor. (Present participle)
> The president *rose* from his chair to greet us. (Past tense)
> The room temperature *has risen* steadily since the meeting began. (Past participle)

The verb *raise* (past tense, *raised;* past participle, *raised*) means "to lift up" or "to elevate" and must have a direct object. The objects in the following sentences have been underlined.

Please *raise* the <u>blinds</u> after the presentation. (Present tense)
The manufacturer *is raising* <u>prices</u> next month. (Present participle)
Dell *raised* its computer <u>prices</u> last month. (Past tense)
She *hasn't raised* the <u>issue</u> yet with her supervisor. (Past participle)

You are now ready to complete the reinforcement exercises.

HOTLINE QUERIES

Q: **I don't have a dictionary handy. Can you tell me which word I should use in this sentence?** *A [stationary/ stationery] circuit board will be installed.*

A: In your sentence use *stationary,* which means "not moving" or "permanent" (*she exercises on a stationary bicycle*). *Stationery* means "writing paper" (*his stationery has his address printed on it*). You might be able to remember the word *stationery* by associating *envelopes* with the *e* in *stationery.*

Q: **I thought I knew the difference between** *principal* **and** *principle,* **but now I'm not so sure. In a report I'm typing** I find this: *The principal findings of the research are negative.* **I thought principal always meant your "pal," the school principal.**

A: You're partly right and partly wrong. *Principal* may be used as a noun meaning "chief" or "head person." In addition, it may be used as an adjective to mean "chief" or "main." This is the meaning most people forget, and this is the meaning of the word in your sentence. The word *principle* means a "law" or "rule." Perhaps it is easiest to remember *princip<u>le</u> = ru<u>le</u>.* All other uses require *principal:* the *principal* of the school, the *principal* of the loan, the *principal* reason.

Q: **Even when I use a dictionary, I can't tell the difference between *affect* and *effect*. What should the word be in this sentence? *Changes in personnel (affected/effected) our production this month.***

A: No words generate more confusion than do *affect* and *effect*. In your sentence use *affected*. Let's see if we can resolve the *affect/effect* dilemma. *Affect* is a verb meaning "to influence" (*smoking affects health; government policies affect citizens*). *Affect* may also mean "to pretend or imitate" (*he affected a British accent*). *Effect* can be a noun or a verb. As a noun, it means "result" (*the effect of the law is slight*). As a verb (and here's the troublesome part) *effect* means "to produce a result" (*small cars effect gasoline savings; GM effected a new pricing policy*).

Q: **I learned that the verb *set* requires an object. If that's true, how can we say that the sun *sets* in the west?**

A: Good question! The verb *set* generally requires an object, but it does have some standardized uses that do not require an object, such as the one you mention. Here's another: *Glue sets up quickly.* I doubt that anyone would be likely to substitute *sit* in either of these unusual situations. While we're on the subject, the verb *sit* also has some exceptions. Although generally the verb *sit* requires no object, *sit* has a few uses that require objects: *Sit yourself down* and *The waiter sat us at Table 1.*

Q: **One of my favorite words is *hopefully*, but I understand that it's often used improperly. How should it be used?**

A: Language purists insist that the word *hopefully* be used to modify a verb (*We looked at the door hopefully, expecting Mr. Guerrero to return momentarily*). The word *hopefully* should not be used as a substitute for *I hope that* or *We hope that*. Instead of saying *Hopefully, interest rates will decline*, one should say *I hope that interest rates will decline*.

Q: **As a command, which is correct: *lay down* or *lie down*?**

A: Commands are given in the present tense. You would never tell someone to *Closed the door*, because commands are not given in the past tense. To say *Lay down* (which is the past tense form of *lie*) is the same as saying *Closed the door*. Therefore, use the present tense: *Lie down*.

Q: **When do you use *may* and when do you use *can*?**

A: Traditionally, the verb *may* is used in asking or granting permission (*yes, you may use that desk*). *Can* is used to suggest ability (*you can succeed in business*). In informal writing, however, authorities today generally agree that *can* may be substituted for *may*.

Q: What's the correct verb in this sentence? *Tim recognized that, if his company (was or were) to prosper, it would require considerable capital.*

A: The verb should be *were* because the clause in which it functions is not true. Statements contrary to fact that are introduced by words like *if* and *wish* require subjunctive mood verbs.

Q: On my computer I'm using a program that checks the writer's style. My problem is that it flags every passive-voice verb and tells me to consider using active-voice verbs. Are passive-voice verbs totally forbidden in business writing?

A: Of course not! Computer style checkers capitalize on language areas that can be detected mechanically, and a passive-voice verb is easily identified by a computer. Although active-voice verbs are considered more forceful, passive-voice verbs have a genuine function in business writing. Because they hide the subject and diffuse attention, passive verbs are useful in sensitive messages where indirect language can develop an impersonal, inconspicuous tone. For example, when a lower-level employee must write a persuasive and somewhat negative message to a manager, passive-voice verbs are quite useful.

Q: My son is studying a foreign language; and he asked me, an English teacher, why we capitalize the personal pronoun *I* in English when we don't capitalize other pronouns.

A: That's a fascinating topic, and a little research on the Web revealed that linguists ponder the same question. In a linguistic journal they discussed some relevant theories. One linguist thought that perhaps the lowercase *i* was too easily confused with the number *1* or with similar looking *i*'s, *u*'s, and *v*'s in medieval handwriting. Another attributed the word's capital letter to our egocentric nature. Another suggested that since the pronoun *I* usually appeared as the first word in a sentence, it was capitalized for that reason. In earlier centuries before the language was standardized, most nouns and pronouns were capitalized haphazardly. One linguist thought that a better question to ask would be why all of the other pronouns lost their capital letters and *I* retained its.

5

VERB AND SUBJECT AGREEMENT

OBJECTIVES

When you have completed the material in this chapter, you will be able to do the following:

- Locate the subjects of verbs despite intervening elements and inverted sentence structure.
- Make verbs agree with true subjects.
- Make verbs agree with subjects joined by *and*.
- Make verbs agree with subjects joined by *or* or *nor*.
- Select the correct verbs to agree with company names, publication titles, collective nouns, and indefinite pronouns.
- Make verbs agree with quantities, fractions, portions, clauses, and *a number/the number*.
- Achieve verb–subject agreement within *who* clauses.

SPOT THE BLOOPER

On the label of Heinz 57 sauce: "Its' unique tangy blend of herbs and spices bring out the natural taste of steak." (Did you spot two bloopers?)

Subjects must agree with verbs in number and person. Beginning a sentence with *He don't* damages a speaker's credibility and limits a communicator's effectiveness.

If an error is made in verb–subject agreement, it can generally be attributed to one of three lapses: (a) failure to locate the subject, (b) failure to recognize the number (singular or plural) of the subject after locating it, or (c) failure to recognize the number of the verb. Suggestions for locating the true subject and determining the number of the subject and its verb follow.

SPOT THE BLOOPER

From a bag of Lay's potato chips: "The great taste of your favorite LAY's flavors are just around the corner."

LOCATING SUBJECTS

All verbs have subjects. Locating these subjects can be difficult, particularly when (a) a prepositional phrase comes between the verb and its subject, (b) an intervening element separates the subject and verb, (c) sentences begin with *there* or *here,* and (d) sentences are inverted.

SPOT THE BLOOPER

Newsweek reported that a child-advocacy group "argues that the use of computers have no proven positive effect on children."

Prepositional Phrases

Subjects of verbs are not found in prepositional phrases. Therefore, you must learn to ignore such phrases in identifying subjects of verbs. Some of the most common prepositions are *of, to, in, from, for, with, at,* and *by.* Notice in the following sentences that the italicized prepositional phrases do not contain the subjects of the verbs.

Each *of our products* is unconditionally guaranteed. (The verb *is* agrees with its singular subject, *each.*)

It appears that the invoice *for the two shipments* was lost. (The verb *was* agrees with its singular subject *invoice.*)

The online version *of the magazine's college rankings* is available at its Web site. (The verb *is* agrees with its subject *version.*)

Some of the less easily recognized prepositions are *except, but, like,* and *between.* In the following sentences, distinguish the subjects from the italicized prepositional phrases.

All employees *but Dierdre* are to report early. (The verb *are* agrees with its plural subject, *employees.*)

Everyone *except the supervisors* is expected to attend. (The verb *is* agrees with its singular subject, *everyone.*)

Intervening Elements

Groups of words introduced by *as well as, in addition to, such as, including, together with,* and *other than* do NOT contain sentence subjects.

Our favorite speaker, *in addition to the other presenters,* is scheduled to appear.

In this sentence the writer has elected to emphasize the subject *speaker* and to de-emphasize *other presenters.* The writer could have given equal weight to these elements by writing *Our favorite speaker and other presenters are scheduled to appear.* Notice that the number (singular or plural) of the verb changes when both *speaker* and *presenters* are given equal emphasis.

Our president, *together with her entire staff of employees,* plans to take this Friday off. (The singular subject *president* agrees with the singular verb *plans.*)

Some entrepreneurs *such as Bill Gates* have started companies based on a single idea. (The plural subject *entrepreneurs* agrees with the plural verb *have.*)

The priceless book, *as well as other valuable documents,* was lost in the fire.

The Adverbs *there* and *here*

In sentences beginning with *there* or *here,* look for the true subject *after* the verb. As adverbs, *here* and *there* cannot function as subjects.

There are many ways to approach the problem. (The plural subject *ways* follows the verb *are.*)

Here is the fuel oil consumption report. (The singular subject *report* follows the verb *is.*)

Be especially careful when using contractions. Remember that *here's* is the contraction for *here is;* therefore, it should be used only with singular subjects. Likewise, *there's* is the contraction for *there is* and should also be used only with singular subjects.

INCORRECT: Here's the documents you requested. (The plural subject *documents* does not agree with the verb *is.*)

CORRECT: Here are the documents you requested. (The plural subject *documents* agrees with the verb *are.*)

INCORRECT: <u>There's</u> three <u>reasons</u> you should hire me for the proofreader position. (The plural subject *reasons* does not agree with the verb *is*.)

CORRECT: There <u>are</u> three <u>reasons</u> you should hire me for the proofreader position. (The plural subject *reasons* agrees with the verb *are*.)

Inverted Sentence Order

Look for the subject after the verb in inverted sentences and in questions.

On our board of directors <u>are</u> three prominent <u>scientists</u>. (Verb precedes subject.)

<u>Have</u> the product <u>specifications</u> <u>been submitted</u>? (Subject separates verb phrase.)

How important <u>are</u> <u>salary</u>, <u>benefits</u>, and <u>job security</u>? (Verb precedes subjects.)

How <u>do</u> <u>law</u> and <u>ethics</u> relate to everyday business? (Verb precedes subjects.)

RULES FOR VERB–SUBJECT AGREEMENT

Once you have located the sentence subject, decide whether the subject is singular or plural and select a verb that agrees in number.

Subjects Joined by *and*

When one subject is joined to another by the word *and,* the subject is plural and requires a plural verb.

<u>Michael Dell</u> and <u>Carly Fiorina</u> <u>are</u> two influential people in the world of technology.

The proposed <u>law</u> and its <u>amendment</u> <u>are</u> before the legislature.

Subjects Joined by *or* or *nor*

When two or more subjects are joined by *or* or *nor,* the verb should agree with the closer subject (the subject that follows *or* or *nor*).

Neither the webmaster nor the <u>clerks</u> <u>know</u> the customer's password.

Neither the clerks nor the <u>webmaster</u> <u>knows</u> the customer's password.

Either Brian or <u>you</u> <u>are</u> in charge of ordering supplies.

Either you or <u>Brian</u> <u>is</u> in charge of ordering supplies.

Either the mayor or his <u>constituents</u> <u>were</u> bound to be unhappy with the results.

Company Names and Titles

Even though they may appear to be plural, company names and titles of publications are singular; therefore, they require singular verbs.

<u>Seven Secrets to Successful Investing</u> <u>is</u> an instant bestseller.

<u>JetBlue Airways</u> <u>is</u> advertising the lowest fare to Washington, D.C.

<u>Milberg; Weiss, and Lerach, Inc.,</u> <u>is</u> offering the bond issue.

Indefinite Pronouns as Subjects

As you may recall from Chapter 3, some indefinite pronouns are always singular, whereas other indefinite pronouns are always plural. In addition, some may be singular or plural depending on the words to which they refer.

	Always Singular			Always Plural	Singular or Plural
anyone	every	nobody		both	all
anybody	everyone	nothing		few	more
anything	everybody	someone		many	most
each	everything	somebody		several	some
either	many a	something			any
	neither				none

Either of the two candidates is qualified.

Everybody in the large group of candidates has an equal chance.

Many of the employees are attending the seminar.

Neither of the Web sites is particularly helpful.

Indefinite pronouns such as *all, more,* and *most* provide one of the few instances in which prepositional phrases become important in determining agreement. Although the prepositional phrase does not contain the subject of the sentence, it does contain the noun to which the indefinite pronoun refers.

Most of the applicants are women. (*Most* is plural because it refers to *applicants.*)

Most of the work is completed. (*Most* is singular because it refers to *work.*)

If the indefinite pronouns *each, every,* or *many a* are used to describe two or more subjects joined by *and,* the subjects are considered separate. Therefore, the verb is singular.

Many a semicolon and colon is misused.

Every man, woman, and child is affected by the tax relief bill.

The indefinite pronouns *anyone, everyone,* and *someone* should be spelled as two words when followed by *of* phrases.

Every one of us should commit to learning the new software package.

Any one of those Web sites can give us the information we need.

Collective Nouns as Subjects

Words such as *faculty, committee,* and *council* may be singular or plural depending on their mode of operation. When a collective noun operates as a single unit, its verb should be singular. When the elements of a collective noun operate separately, the verb should be plural.

Our staff has unanimously adopted the board's proposal. (*Staff* is acting as a single unit.)

The council were sharply divided over the budget. (*Council* members were acting separately. While technically correct, the sentence would be less awkward if it read *The council members were sharply . . .*)

The Distinction Between *the number* and *a number*

When the word *number* is the subject of a sentence, its article (*the* or *a*) becomes significant. *The* is specific and therefore implies *singularity; a* is general and therefore implies *plurality.*

The number of requests for registered domain names is growing annually. (Singular)

A number of stocks are traded daily. (Plural)

Quantities, Measures

When quantities and measures refer to *total* amounts, they are singular. If they refer to individual units that can be counted, quantities and measures are plural.

> Five years is the period of the loan. (Quantity as a total amount)
> Five days are required to complete the project. (Quantity as individual units)

Fractions, Portions

Fractions and portions may be singular or plural depending on the nouns to which they refer.

> Only a third of the students' reading scores are satisfactory. (The fraction *third* is plural because it refers to *scores*.)
>
> Over half of the contract was ratified. (The fraction *half* is singular because it refers to *contract*.)
>
> A majority of employees agree with the proposal. (The portion *majority* is plural because it refers to *employees*.)
>
> A percentage of the budget is allocated to employee benefits. (The subject *percentage* is singular because it refers to *budget*.)
>
> A percentage of the proceeds go to charity. (The subject *percentage* is plural because it refers to *proceeds*.)
>
> Part of the proposal is ambiguous. (The subject *part* is plural because it refers to *proposal*.)

Who Clauses

STUDY TIP ▼

For sentences with *one of those who* clauses, begin reading with the word *of: Of those people who give 100 percent, Richard is one.* The verb will always be plural. However, if the sentence is limited by *only one*, the verb is always singular.

Verbs in *who* clauses must agree in number and person with the nouns to which they refer. In *who* clauses introduced by *one of*, the verb is usually plural because it refers to a plural antecedent. In *who* clauses introduced by *the only one of*, the verb is singular.

> Richard is *one of* those people who always give 100 percent. (Read: Of those people who always give 100 percent, Richard is one.)
>
> Sandy Collins is *one of* those managers who always get excellent results from their employees. (Read: Of those managers who always get excellent results from their employees, Sandy Collins is one. Note that the pronoun *their* also must agree with its antecedent.)
>
> Don is *the only one of* our employees who is trained in Web page design. (The adverb *only* limits the number to one.)

Verbs must agree in person with the nouns or pronouns to which they refer.

> It is you who are responsible for security.
> Could it be I who am to blame?
> Was it you who were on the phone?

SPOT THE BLOOPER

Headline from the Santa Barbara [California] *News-Press:* "Adding Rental Units Transform Home."

Phrases and Clauses as Subjects

Use a singular verb when the subject of a sentence is a phrase or clause.

> Learning about the stock market is fascinating.
> Relying too much on others is detrimental.

Subject Complements

In Chapter 4 you learned that linking verbs are followed by complements. Although a complement may differ from the subject in number, the linking verb should always agree with the subject. To avoid awkwardness, reword sentences so that subjects and complements agree in number.

AWKWARD: The best <u>part</u> of the Web site <u>is</u> the <u>graphics and video</u>. (Although the singular subject *part* agrees with the singular verb *is,* it sounds awkward because of the plural complement *graphics and video*.)

BETTER: The best <u>parts</u> of the Web site <u>are</u> the <u>graphics and video</u>. (The plural subject agrees with the plural complement.)

AWKWARD: The <u>reason</u> for his bankruptcy <u>was</u> poor <u>investments</u> in stocks.

BETTER: The <u>reasons</u> for his bankruptcy <u>were</u> poor <u>investments</u> in stocks.

You are now ready to complete the reinforcement exercises.

HOTLINE QUERIES

Q: My uncle insists that *none* is singular. My English book says that it can be plural. Who's right?

A: Times are changing. Thirty years ago *none* was almost always used in a singular sense. Today, through usage, *none* may be singular or plural depending on what you wish to emphasize. For example, *None are more willing than we.* But, *None of the students is* (or *are* if you wish to suggest many students) *failing.*

Q: When do you use *all together,* and when do you use *altogether?*

A: *All together* means "collectively" or "all the members of a group" (*we must work all together to reach our goal*). *Altogether* means "entirely" (*he was altogether satisfied*).

Q: Please help me with this sentence that I'm transcribing for a medical laboratory: *A copy of our analysis, along* *with our interpretation of its results, (has or have) been sent to you.*

A: The subject of your sentence is *copy*; thus the verb must be *has*. Don't let interrupting elements obscure the real sentence subject.

Q: After looking in the dictionary, I'm beginning to wonder about this: *We have alot of work yet to do.* I can't find the word *alot* in the dictionary, but it must be there. Everyone uses it.

A: The two-word phrase *a lot* is frequently used in conversation or in very informal writing (*the copier makes a lot of copies*). *Alot* as one word does not exist. Don't confuse it with *allot* meaning "to distribute" (*the company will allot to each department its share of supplies*).

Q: Should *reevaluate* be hyphenated?

A: No. It is not necessary to use a hyphen after the prefix *re* unless the resulting word may be confused with another word (*to re-mark the sales ticket, to re-cover the chair*).

Q: I'm totally confused by job titles for women today. What do I call a woman who is a *fireman, a policeman, a chairman,* **or a** *spokesman?* **And what about the word** *mankind?*

A: As more and more women enter nontraditional careers, some previous designations are being replaced by neutral, inclusive titles. Here are some substitutes:

actor	for *actress*
firefighter	for *fireman*
mail carrier	for *mailman*
police officer	for *policeman*
flight attendant	for *steward* or *stewardess*
reporter or journalist	for *newsman*
server	for *waiter* or *waitress*

Words like *chairman, spokesman,* and *mankind* traditionally have been used to refer to both men and women. Today, though, sensitive writers strive to use more inclusive language. Possible substitutes are *chair, spokesperson,* and *humanity.*

Q: I'm never sure how to handle words that are used to represent quantities and proportions in sentences. For example, what verb is correct in this sentence *A large proportion of voters (was or were) against the measure.*

A: Words that represent fractional amounts (such as *proportion, fraction, minimum,* and *majority*) may be singular or plural depending on the words they represent. In your sentence *proportion* represents *voters,* which is plural. Therefore, use the plural verb *were.*

Q: **In a recent *Wall Street Journal* article, I saw this sentence: *At issue is other tax breaks, especially Hope and Lifetime Learning education tax credits.* I don't usually question the *Journal,* but this sentence is weird. What is its problem?**

A: Because the sentence order is inverted, the writer had trouble making the subject and verb agree. By moving the subject to the beginning, you can see that it is plural. And a plural subject always demands a plural verb: *Other tax breaks . . . are at issue.*

Q: **I have a lot of trouble with verbs in sentences like this:**

He is one of the 8 million Americans who (has or have) a drinking problem.

A: You're not alone. Make your verb agree with its antecedent (*Americans*). One easy way to work with sentences like this is to concentrate on the clause that contains the verb: *Of the 8 million Americans who have a drinking problem, he is one.*

Q: **In a *New York Times* article about singer Michael Jackson and his fight with Sony Music Group, I saw this sentence: *Owning those rights are valuable because once Mr. Jackson owns them outright, he does not have to split royalty payments with Sony as he does now.* It seems to me the phrase *owning those rights* is singular and the verb should be *is.* Am I right?**

A: Absolutely! When they act as sentence subjects, phrases and clauses are singular. You deserve a good grammar award!

InfoTrac Activity

InfoTrac in Action

Using an InfoTrac keyword search, find an article titled "Word-Usage Rules for Writing  Strong Memos & Reports." In the space provided or in a memo to your instructor, briefly summarize the article and answer these questions: What kind of verbs give your writing power? How can verbs be "buried"? Give several examples. What's wrong with passive verbs? Why should linking verbs be treated carefully?

6

VERBALS

OBJECTIVES

When you have completed the material in this chapter, you will be able to do the following:

- Recognize gerunds and supply appropriate modifiers of gerunds.
- Identify and remedy split infinitives that result in awkward sentences.
- Avoid writing awkward participial phrases.
- Correctly punctuate introductory and other verbal phrases.
- Spot dangling verbal phrases and other misplaced modifiers.
- Rewrite sentences to avoid misplaced verbal phrases and modifiers.

As you learned earlier, English is a highly flexible language in which a given word may have more than one grammatical function. In this chapter you will study verbals. Derived from verbs, *verbals* are words that function as nouns, adjectives, or adverbs. Three kinds of verbals are gerunds (verbal nouns), infinitives, and participles (verbal adjectives).

STUDY TIP▼

To distinguish between *ing* forms used as nouns and those used as adjectives, try the *what?* question approach. In the sentence *I admired Sara's programming,* say to yourself, "I admired what?" Answer: "I admired Sara's *programming,* not Sara." Therefore, *programming* is the object and functions as an *ing* noun.

SPOT THE BLOOPER

From a notice to holders of Exxon credit cards: "We appreciate you choosing Exxon . . ."

SPOT THE BLOOPER

From *The Boston Globe:* "Equity-stripping could result in you losing your home."

GERUNDS

A verb form ending in *ing* and used as a noun is called a *gerund.*

> *Marketing* our product on the Web is necessary. (Gerund used as the subject)
> Amarjit enjoys *snowboarding.* (Gerund used as the direct object)

Using Gerunds Correctly

In using gerunds, follow this rule: Make any noun or pronoun modifying a gerund possessive, as in *Karen's procrastinating* or *Dale's computing.* Because we sometimes fail to recognize gerunds as nouns, we fail to make their modifiers possessive:

> WRONG: The staff objects to *Kevin smoking.*
> RIGHT: The staff objects to *Kevin's smoking.*

The staff does not object to Kevin, as the first version states; it objects to his smoking. If we substitute a more easily recognized noun for *smoking,* the possessive form seems more natural: *The staff objects to Kevin's behavior. Behavior* is a noun, just as *smoking* is a noun; the noun or pronoun modifiers of both must be possessive.

> The manager appreciated *his* working late. (The gerund *working* requires the possessive pronoun *his,* not the objective-case pronoun *him.*)
> I resent *your calling* during my lunch hour. (Not *you calling*)

Not all verbs ending in *ing* are, of course, gerunds. Some are elements in verb phrases and some act as adjectives. Compare these three sentences:

I saw Kelli negotiating. (The word *negotiating* functions as an adjective describing Kelli.)

I admired Kelli's negotiating. (As the object of the verb, *negotiating* acts as a gerund.)

Kelli is negotiating. (Here *is negotiating* is a verb phrase.)

INFINITIVES

When the present form of a verb is preceded by *to,* the most basic verb form results: the *infinitive.* The sign of the infinitive is the word *to.*

She tried *to follow* your instructions exactly.

To write clearly and concisely requires great skill.

Using Infinitives Correctly

In certain expressions infinitives may be misused. Observe the use of the word *to* in the following infinitive phrases. Do not substitute the conjunction *and* for the *to* of the infinitive.

Try *to call* when you arrive. (Not *try and call*)

Be sure *to speak* softly when you use your cell phone in public. (Not *be sure and speak*)

Check *to see* when the flight is due to arrive. (Not *check and see*)

When any word appears between *to* and the verb (*to* carefully *prepare*), an infinitive is said to be split. At one time split infinitives were considered great grammatical sins. Today most authorities agree that infinitives may be split if necessary for clarity and effect. Avoid, however, split infinitives that result in awkward sentences.

AWKWARD: Neal Skapura wanted *to,* if he could find time, *recheck* his figures.

BETTER: If he could find time, Neal Skapura wanted *to recheck* his figures.

AWKWARD: Our company has *to,* when the real estate market returns to normal, *consider* purchasing an office building.

BETTER: Our company has *to consider,* when the real estate market returns to normal, purchasing an office building.

ACCEPTABLE: *To* honestly *state* the facts is the job of the prosecutor. (No awkwardness results from split infinitive.)

ACCEPTABLE: In an attempt to attract new customers, the company decided *to* aggressively *market* its products. (No awkwardness results from split infinitive.)

PARTICIPLES

You have already studied the present and past forms of participles functioning as parts of verb phrases. You will recall that in such constructions present and past participles always require helping verbs: *is working, was seen, had broken.*

In this chapter we are concerned with a second possible function of participles. Participles can function as adjectives. As adjectives, participles modify nouns or pronouns, and they do not require helping verbs.

Here are sentences that illustrate the five forms of the participle.

Present participle, active: *Helping Ben with the proposal,* we all decided to work late. (The participial phrase *helping Ben with the proposal* modifies *we.*)

Present participle, passive: Ben Seaberry, *being helped by his colleagues,* is completing the proposal. (*Being helped by his colleagues* is a participial phrase that describes *Ben Seaberry.*)

Past participle, passive: Although *helped by three others,* Ben found it difficult to meet the deadline. (The participial phrase *helped by three others* functions as an adjective to describe *Ben.*)

Perfect participle, active: *Having helped Ben* on many previous occasions, his colleagues knew that somehow they would accomplish their goals. (The participial phrase *Having helped Ben* describes *his colleagues.*)

Perfect participle, passive: Ben, *having been helped* on many big projects, was deeply indebted to his colleagues. (The participial phrase *having been helped* functions as an adjective to describe *Ben.*)

Using Participles Correctly

Avoid using participial phrases that sound awkward, such as these:

AWKWARD: Kristi's having been promoted to office manager was cause for celebration.

BETTER: Kristi's promotion to office manager was cause for celebration.

AWKWARD: Being as you live nearby, should we carpool?

BETTER: Since you live nearby, should we carpool?

PUNCTUATING VERBAL FORMS

Determining whether verbal forms require commas often causes difficulty. Let's try to clear up this difficulty with explanations and examples.

Punctuating Introductory Verbal Forms

When verbal forms are used in introductory words or expressions, there's no question about punctuating them. A comma should be placed between an introductory verbal form and the main clause of a sentence.

Astonished, the attorney turned to the jury. (Introductory verbal form)

To raise funds for charity, Berkshire Hathaway offered a lunch with Warren Buffett as an auction item on eBay. (Introductory verbal phrase)

Receiving too many e-mail messages, Paul Nilsen established filters. (Introductory verbal phrase)

Completing 43 years of service, Lynn Reynolds retired. (Introductory verbal phrase)

Not all verbal phrases that begin sentences, however, are considered introductory. If the verbal phrase represents the subject or part of the predicate of the sentence, NO comma should separate it from the rest of the sentence.

Preparing a budget is Andy's responsibility. (Verbal phrase used as subject; no comma)

To change the schedule at this point would be difficult. (Verbal phrase used as subject; no comma)

Offering stock options is one way to motivate workers. (Verbal phrase used as part of predicate; no comma)

Punctuating Nonessential Verbal Phrases*

Essential (restrictive) information is needed for the reader to understand the sentence. Verbal phrases often help identify the subject. These phrases require no commas. Nonessential information could be omitted without altering the basic meaning of the sentence; thus nonessential phrases are set off by commas.

Cheryl Martucci, *working late at the office,* was able to meet the deadline. (The verbal phrase *working late at the office* adds additional information, but it is not essential. The subject is fully identified by name. Use commas to set off the nonessential phrase.)

The woman *working late at the office* was able to meet the deadline. (In this sentence the verbal phrase *working late at the office* is essential; it is needed to identify the subject. *Which* woman was able to meet the deadline? The woman *working late at the office.* No commas separate this essential verbal phrase.)

CitiBank, *opening a new branch in San Antonio,* offered free online banking to attract customers. (The verbal phrase is not essential because there is only one CitiBank, and it has been identified. Commas enclose this nonessential verbal phrase.)

A bank *opening a new branch in San Antonio* offered free online banking to attract customers. (This verbal phrase is essential to identify *which* bank offered free online banking. No commas are needed. **Note:** Even though you pause when you reach the end of the verbal phrase, don't be tempted to add a comma.)

Notice in the preceding sentences that whenever a nonessential verbal phrase interrupts the middle of a sentence, two commas set it off.

AVOIDING MISPLACED VERBAL MODIFIERS

Introductory Verbal Phrases

Introductory verbal phrases must be followed by the words they can logically modify. Such phrases can create confusion or unintended humor when placed incorrectly in a sentence. Consider this sentence: *Sitting in the car, the mountains were breathtaking.* The introductory participial phrase in this sentence is said to *dangle* because it is not followed immediately by a word it can logically modify. The sentence could be improved by revising it to read: *Sitting in the car, we saw the breathtaking mountains.* Observe how the following illogical sentences have been improved:

ILLOGICAL: Slipping on the stairs, his back was injured.

LOGICAL: Slipping on the stairs, *he* injured his back.

ILLOGICAL: Turning on the fan, papers flew about the office.

LOGICAL: Turning on the fan, *I* caused papers to fly about the office.

ILLOGICAL: To receive a free DVD, the enclosed card must be returned.

LOGICAL: To receive a free DVD, you must return the enclosed card.

---

*Many people find it easier to work with the words *essential* and *nonessential* than with the more traditional grammatical terms *restrictive* and *nonrestrictive;* therefore, the easier terminology is used here.

ILLOGICAL:	Skilled with computers, the recruiter hired Ruth Sison.
LOGICAL:	Skilled with computers, Ruth Sison was hired by the recruiter
BUT:	To master a language, listen carefully to native speakers.
	To master a language, (you) listen carefully to native speakers. (In commands, the understood subject is *you*. Therefore, this sentence is correctly followed by the word to which it refers.)

Verbal Phrases in Other Positions

In other positions within sentences, verbal phrases must also be placed in logical relation to the words they modify.

ILLOGICAL:	The missing purchase orders were found by Laurie Lema's secretary lying in her top desk drawer.
LOGICAL:	Laurie Lema's secretary found the missing purchase orders lying in her top desk drawer.
ILLOGICAL:	Doctors discovered that his ankle had been fractured in five places during surgery.
LOGICAL:	During surgery, doctors discovered that his ankle had been fractured in five places.

You are now ready to complete the reinforcement exercises.

HOTLINE QUERIES

Q: I saw this in an auction announcement for a Beverly Hills home: *Married to interior decorator Dusty Bartlett, their home saw many of the great Hollywood parties with friends such as Ingrid Bergmann and Katharine Hepburn setting by the pool on weekends.* Am I just imagining, or does this sentence say that the home was married to the interior decorator?

A: Amazing, isn't it! But that's what the sentence says. This is a classic misplaced modifier. An introductory verbal phrase must be immediately followed by words that the phrase can logically modify. This sentence doesn't give us a clue. Did you also notice another problem? The verb *setting* should be *sitting*.

HOTLINE QUERIES

Q: Are there two meanings for the word *discreet?*

A: You are probably confusing the two words *discreet* and *discrete*. *Discreet* means "showing good judgment" and "prudent" (*the witness gave a discreet answer, avoiding gossip and hearsay*). The word *discrete* means "separate" or "noncontinuous" (*Alpha, Inc., has installed discrete computers rather than a network computer system*). You might find it helpful to remember that the *e*'s are separate in *discrete.*

Q: Should I use *complimentary* or *complementary* to describe free tickets?

A: Use *complimentary,* which can mean "containing a compliment, favorable, or free" (*the dinner came with complimentary wine; he made a complimentary remark*). *Complementary* means "completing or making perfect" (*the complementary colors enhanced the room*). An easy way to remember *compliment* is by thinking "*I* like to receive a compl*i*ment."

Q: I confuse *i.e.* and *e.g.* What's the difference?

A: The abbreviation *i.e.* stands for the Latin *id est,* meaning "that is" (*the package exceeds the weight limit, i.e., 5 pounds*). Notice the use of a comma after *i.e.* The abbreviation *e.g.* stands for the Latin *exempli*

gratia, meaning "for the sake of example" or "for example" (*the manufacturer may offer a purchase incentive, e.g., a rebate or discount plan*).

Q: I'm not sure which word to use in this sentence: *They have used all (they're, their, there) resources in combating the disease.*

A: Use *their,* which is the possessive form of *they.* The adverb *there* means "at that place or at that point" (*we have been there before*). *There* is also used as an expletive or filler preceding a linking verb (*there are numerous explanations*). *They're* is a contraction of *they* and *are* (*they're coming this afternoon*).

Q: In a letter written by my boss, how should we spell *there? We do not want an open invoice without there being justifiable reasons.*

A: *There* is spelled correctly, but its use creates an awkward verbal form. If your boss agrees, revise the sentence to read*: We do not want an open invoice without justification.*

Q: What's the difference between *toward* and *towards?*

A: None. They are interchangeable in use. However, it's more efficient to use the shorter word *toward.*

MODIFYING AND CONNECTING WORDS

MODIFIERS: ADJECTIVES AND ADVERBS

OBJECTIVES

When you have completed the material in this chapter, you will be able to do the following:

- Form the comparative and superlative degrees of regular and irregular adjectives and adverbs.
- Use articles correctly and avoid double negatives.
- Use adjectives after linking verbs and use adverbs to modify verbs, adjectives, and other adverbs.
- Punctuate compound and successive independent adjectives correctly.
- Compare degrees of absolute adjectives and make comparisons within a group.
- Place adverbs and adjectives close to the words they modify.

SPOT THE BLOOPER

From a job applicant's cover letter: "I'm often described as out going."

Both adjectives and adverbs act as modifiers; that is, they describe or limit other words. Many of the forms and functions of adjectives and adverbs are similar. Because of this similarity, these two parts of speech may be confused. That's why we will treat adjectives and adverbs together in this chapter.

BASIC FUNCTIONS OF ADJECTIVES AND ADVERBS

Adjectives describe or limit nouns and pronouns. They often answer the questions *what kind? how many?* or *which one?* Adjectives in the following sentences are italicized. Observe that the adjectives all answer questions about the nouns they describe.

SPOT THE BLOOPER

The menu of a restaurant in Columbia, South Carolina, offers "A humongous baked potato, slightly hallowed and stuffed."

Small, independent businesses are becoming *numerous.* (What kinds of businesses?)
We have *six* franchises in *four* states. (How many franchises? How many states?)
That chain of hotels started as a *small* operation. (Which chain? What kind of operation?)
He is *energetic* and *forceful,* whereas she is *personable* and *deliberate.* (What pronouns do these adjectives describe?)

SPOT THE BLOOPER

From *The Wall Street Journal* comes a report that Marshall Field's, the big Chicago retailer, announced it would serve hot chocolate to "tiresome" shoppers.

Adjectives usually precede nouns. They may, however, follow the words they describe, especially when used with linking verbs, as shown in the first and last of the previous examples. Here is a brief list of words often used as adjectives:

dynamic	long	small
effective	professional	successful
intelligent	responsible	yellow

Adverbs describe or limit verbs, adjectives, or other adverbs. They often answer the questions *when? how? where?* or *to what extent?*

He seemed *exceedingly* competent. (How competent?)
Today we left work *early.* (Left when? How?)
You may have a seat *there.* (Where?)
The prosecutor did not question him *further.* (Questioned him to what extent?)

Here are additional examples of common adverbs:

again	much	rather	tomorrow
always	never	really	too
carefully	not	seldom	very
finally	now	so	well
here	often	sometimes	what
indeed	only	soon	when
later	probably	still	where

Many, but not all, words ending in *ly* are adverbs. Some exceptions are *friendly, costly,* and *ugly,* all of which are adjectives.

Comparative and Superlative Forms

Most adjectives and adverbs have three forms, or degrees: positive, comparative, and superlative. The following examples illustrate how the comparative and superlative degrees of regular adjectives and adverbs are formed.

	POSITIVE	COMPARATIVE	SUPERLATIVE
ADJECTIVE:	warm	warmer	warmest
ADVERB:	warmly	more/less warmly	most/least warmly
ADJECTIVE:	easy	easier	easiest
ADVERB:	easily	more/less easily	most/least easily
ADJECTIVE:	careful	more/less careful	most/least careful
ADVERB:	carefully	more/less carefully	most/least carefully

The positive degree of an adjective or an adverb is used in merely describing or in limiting another word. The comparative degree is used to compare two persons or things. The superlative degree is used in the comparison of three or more persons or things.

The comparative degree of short adjectives (nearly all one-syllable and most two-syllable adjectives ending in *y)* is formed by adding *r* or *er* (*warmer*). The superlative degree of short adjectives is formed by the addition of *st* or *est* (*warmest*). Long adjectives, and those difficult to pronounce, form the comparative and superlative degrees, as do adverbs, with the addition of *more* and *most* (*more careful, most beautiful*) or *less* and *least* (*less careful, least careful*). The following sentences illustrate degrees of comparison for adjectives and adverbs.

ADJECTIVES:	Sales are unusually *high.*	(Positive degree)
	Sales are *higher* than ever before.	(Comparative degree)
	Sales are the *highest* in years.	(Superlative degree)
ADVERBS:	He works *quickly.*	(Positive degree)
	He works *more quickly* than his partner.	(Comparative degree)
	He works *most quickly* under pressure.	(Superlative degree)

Do not create a double comparative form by using *more* and the suffix *er* together (such as *more neater*) or by using *most* and the suffix *est* together (such as *most fastest*).

A few adjectives and adverbs form the comparative and superlative degrees irregularly.

	POSITIVE	COMPARATIVE	SUPERLATIVE
ADJECTIVE:	good	better	best
ADJECTIVE:	well	better	best
ADJECTIVE:	little	less	least
ADJECTIVE:	many, much	more	most
ADVERB:	well	better	best
ADVERB:	much	more	most

MODIFIERS THAT DESERVE SPECIAL ATTENTION

A few adjectives and adverbs require special attention because they cause writers and speakers difficulty.

Adjectives as Articles

The articles *a, an,* and *the* must be used carefully. When describing a specific person or thing, use the article *the,* as in *the firm.* When describing persons or things in general, use *a* or *an,* as in *a firm* (meaning *any* firm). The choice of *a* or *an* is determined by the initial sound of the word modified. *A* is used before consonant sounds; *an* is used before vowel sounds.

BEFORE VOWEL SOUNDS		BEFORE CONSONANT SOUNDS	
an operator		a printer	
an executive		a plan	
an hour } an honor }	*h* is not voiced; vowel is heard	a hook } a hole }	*h* is voiced
an office } an opinion }	*o* sounds like a vowel	a one-year contract } a one-week trip }	*o* sounds like the consonant *w*
an urgent request } an undertaking }	*u* sounds like a vowel	a union } a unit }	*u* sounds like the consonant *y*
an X-ray } an M.D. }	*x* and *m* sound like vowels		

Adverbs and Double Negatives

When a negative adverb (*no, not, nothing, scarcely, hardly, barely*) is used in the same sentence with a negative verb (*didn't, don't, won't*), a substandard construction called a *double negative* results. Among professionals, such constructions are considered to be illogical and illiterate. In the following examples, notice that eliminating one negative corrects the double negative.

INCORRECT:	Calling her *won't* do *no* good.
CORRECT:	Calling her will do no good.
CORRECT:	Calling her won't do any good.

INCORRECT:	We *couldn't hardly* believe the news report.
CORRECT:	We could hardly believe the news report.
CORRECT:	We couldn't believe the news report.
INCORRECT:	Drivers *can't barely* see in the heavy fog.
CORRECT:	Drivers can barely see in the heavy fog.
CORRECT:	Drivers can't see in the heavy fog.
INCORRECT:	He *didn't have nothing* to do with it.
CORRECT:	He had nothing to do with it.
CORRECT:	He didn't have anything to do with it.

The Adjectives *this/that* and *these/those*

The adjective *this,* and its plural form *these,* indicates something nearby. The adjective *that,* and its plural form *those,* indicates something at a distance. Be careful to use the singular forms of these words with singular nouns and the plural forms with plural nouns.

> *This company* looks promising. (Singular)
> *That decision* was necessary. (Singular)
> *These accounts* need attention. (Plural)
> *Those records* are sealed. (Plural)

Pay special attention to the nouns *kind, type,* and *sort.* Match singular adjectives to the singular forms of these nouns.

> *This kind of question* shows careful thought. (Singular)
> *That sort of person* is exactly what this company needs. (Singular)
> *These types of questions* are unnecessary. (Plural)
> *Those sorts of people* should be avoided. (Plural)

CHALLENGES IN USING ADJECTIVES AND ADVERBS

In this discussion you will learn to avoid confusing adjectives with adverbs. You will also learn to express compound adjectives and independent adjectives. Finally, you will learn how to use absolute modifiers, how to make comparisons within a group, and how to place adjectives and adverbs appropriately in sentences.

Confusion of Adjectives and Adverbs

Because they are closely related, adjectives and adverbs are sometimes confused. Here are guidelines that will help you choose the appropriate adjective or adverb.

■ *Use adjectives to modify nouns and pronouns.* Note particularly that adjectives (not adverbs) should follow linking verbs.

> This pasta tastes *delicious.* (Not *deliciously*)
> I feel *bad* about the loss. (Not *badly*)
> He looks *good* in his tuxedo. (Not *well*)

■ *Use adverbs to describe verbs, adjectives, or other adverbs.* Notice that adverbs follow action verbs.

> The engine runs *smoothly.* (Not *smooth*)
> It runs *more smoothly* than before. (Not *smoother*)

Listen *carefully* to the directions. (Not *careful*)
Time passes *quickly*. (Not *quick*)

It should be noted that a few adverbs have two acceptable forms: *slow, slowly; deep, deeply; direct, directly;* and *close, closely.*

Drive *slowly*. (Or, less formally, *slow*)
You may dial us *directly*. (Or, less formally, *direct*)

Compound Adjectives

Writers may form their own adjectives by joining two or more words. When these words act as a single modifier preceding a noun, they are temporarily hyphenated. If these same words appear after a noun, they are generally not hyphenated.

WORDS TEMPORARILY HYPHENATED BEFORE A NOUN	SAME WORDS NOT HYPHENATED AFTER A NOUN
never-say-die attitude	attitude of never say die
eight-story building	building of eight stories
state-sponsored program	program that is state sponsored
a case-by-case analysis	analysis that is case by case
high-performance computer	computer that has high performance
income-related expenses	expenses that are income related
government-subsidized loan	loan that is government subsidized
home-based business	business that is based at home
two-year-old company	company that is two years old

Compound adjectives shown in your dictionary with hyphens are considered permanently hyphenated. Regardless of whether the compound appears before or after a noun, it retains the hyphens. Use a current dictionary to determine what expressions are always hyphenated. Be sure that you find the dictionary entry that is marked *adjective*. Here are samples:

PERMANENT HYPHENS BEFORE NOUNS	PERMANENT HYPHENS AFTER NOUNS
first-class seats	seats that are first-class
up-to-date information	information that is up-to-date
old-fashioned attitude	attitude that is old-fashioned
short-term goals	goals that are short-term
well-known expert	expert who is well-known
out-of-pocket expenses	expenses that are out-of-pocket
part-time employee	employee who is part-time

Don't confuse adverbs ending in *ly* with compound adjectives: *newly appointed judge* and *highly regarded entrepreneur* would not be hyphenated.

As compound adjectives become more familiar, they are often simplified and the hyphen is dropped. Some familiar compounds that are not hyphenated are *high school student, charge account balance, income tax refund, home office equipment, word processing software,* and *data processing center.*

Independent Adjectives

Two or more successive adjectives that independently modify a noun are separated by commas. No comma is needed, however, when the first adjective modifies the combined idea of the second adjective and the noun.

TWO ADJECTIVES INDEPENDENTLY MODIFYING A NOUN	FIRST ADJECTIVE MODIFYING A SECOND ADJECTIVE PLUS A NOUN
productive, reliable employee	efficient administrative assistant
economical, efficient car	graphite grey sports car
stimulating, provocative book	assistant deputy director

Special Cases

The following adjectives and adverbs cause difficulty for some writers and speakers. With a little study, you can master their correct usage.

almost (adv.—nearly): *Almost* (not *Most*) everybody wants to work.

most (adj.—greatest in amount): *Most* people want to work.

farther (adv.—actual distance): How much *farther* is the airport?

further (adv.—additionally): Let's discuss the issue *further.*

sure (adj.—certain): She is *sure* of her decision.

surely (adv.—undoubtedly): He will *surely* be selected for the position.

later (adv.—after expected time): The contract arrived *later* in the day.

latter (adj.—the second of two things): Of the two candidates, I prefer the *latter.*

fewer (adj.—refers to countable numbers): *Fewer* than 50 people applied for the position.

less (adj.—refers to amounts or quantities that cannot be counted): *Less* time remains than we anticipated.

real (adj.—actual, genuine): The *real* power in the company lies with the board of directors.

really (adv.—actually, truly): Jan was *really* eager to take her vacation.

good (adj.—desirable): A number of *good* plans were submitted.

well { (adv.—satisfactorily): Jeff did *well* on his performance evaluation.
{ (adj.—healthy): Jamal feels *well* enough to go back to work.

Absolute Modifiers

Adjectives and adverbs that name perfect or complete (absolute) qualities cannot logically be compared. For example, to say that one ball is more *round* than another ball is illogical. Here are some absolute words that should not be used in comparisons.

round	dead	complete
perfect	true	right
unique	correct	straight
perpendicular	endless	unanimous

Authorities suggest, however, that some absolute adjectives may be compared by the use of the words *more nearly* or *most nearly.*

Ron's account of the proceedings was *more nearly accurate* than Sue's version. (Not *more accurate*)

Kris's project is *more nearly complete* than mine (Not *more complete*)

Comparisons Within a Group

When the word *than* is used to compare a person, place, or thing with other members of a group to which it belongs, be certain to include the words *other* or *else* in the comparison. This inclusion ensures that the person or thing being compared is separated from the group with which it is compared.

ILLOGICAL:	Alaska is larger than any state in the United States. (This sentence suggests that Alaska is larger than itself.)
LOGICAL:	Alaska is larger than any *other* state in the United States.
ILLOGICAL:	Our team had better results than any team in the company.
LOGICAL:	Our team had better results than any *other* team in the company.
ILLOGICAL:	Alex works harder than anyone in the office.
LOGICAL:	Alex works harder than anyone *else* in the office.

SPOT THE BLOOPER

Headline from *The Concord Monitor* [Concord, New Hampshire]: "How Can You Expect a Child Who Can't Tell Time to Only Get Sick During Office Hours?"

Placing Adverbs and Adjectives

The position of an adverb or adjective can seriously affect the meaning of a sentence. Study these examples.

Only Mike Mixon can change the password. (No one else can change it.)
Mike Mixon can *only* change the password. (He can't do anything else to it.)
Mike Mixon can change *only* the password. (He can't change anything else.)

To avoid confusion, adverbs and adjectives should be placed close to the words they modify. In this regard, special attention should be given to the words *only, merely, first,* and *last.*

CONFUSING:	He *merely* said that the report could be improved.
CLEAR:	He said *merely* that the report could be improved.
CONFUSING:	Seats in the five *first* rows have been reserved.
CLEAR:	Seats in the *first* five rows have been reserved.

You are now ready to complete the reinforcement exercises.

HOTLINE QUERIES

Q: My colleague insists that the word *his* is an adjective when it is used in an expression such as *his car.* I learned that *his* was a pronoun. What is it?

A: When words such as *his, her, our, your, their,* and *it* function as adjectives, they are classified as adjectives. Although most people consider them pronouns, when these words describe nouns they are actually functioning as adjectives. Your colleague is right.

Q: Why does the sign above my grocery market's quick-check stand say *Ten or less items?* Shouldn't it read *Ten or fewer items?*

A: Right you are! *Fewer* refers to numbers, as in *fewer items. Less* refers to amounts or quantities, as in *less food.* Perhaps markets prefer *less* because it has fewer letters.

Q: Is it necessary to hyphenate a *25 percent* discount?

A: No. Percents are not treated in the same way that numbers appearing in compound adjectives are treated. Thus, you would not hyphenate a

15 percent loan, but you would hyphenate a *15-year* loan.

Q: Should hyphens be used in *a point-by-point analysis?*

A: Yes. When words are combined to create a single adjective preceding a noun, these words are temporarily hyphenated (*last-minute decision, two-semester course, step-by-step procedures*).

Q: How many hyphens should I use in this sentence? *The three, four, and five year plans continue to be funded.*

A: Three hyphens are needed: *three-, four-, and five-year plans*. Hyphenate compound adjectives even when the parts of the compound are separated or suspended.

Q: I never know how to write *part time.* Is it always hyphenated?

A: The dictionary shows all of its uses to be hyphenated. *She was a part-time employee* (used as an adjective). *He worked part-time* (used as an adverb).

Q: Here are some expressions that caused us trouble in our business letters. We want to hyphenate all of the following. Right? *Well-produced play, awareness-generation film, decision-making tables, one-paragraph note, swearing-in ceremony, commonly-used book.*

A: All your hyphenated forms are correct except the last one. Don't use a hyphen with an *ly*-ending adverb.

Q: Why are these two expressions treated differently: *two-week* vacation and *two weeks'* vacation?

A: Although they express the same idea, they represent two different styles. If you omit the *s, two-week* is hyphenated because it is a compound adjective. If you add the *s,* as in *two weeks' vacation,* the expression becomes possessive and requires an apostrophe. Don't use both styles together (not *two-weeks' vacation*).

Q: Is this a double negative? *We can't schedule the meeting because we have no room available.*

A: No, this is not regarded as a double negative. In grammar a double negative is created when two negative adverbs modify a verb, such as *can't hardly, won't barely,* or *can't help but.* Avoid such constructions.

Q: Which is correct? *I feel (bad or badly)*

A: *Bad* is an adjective meaning "not good" or "ill." *Badly* is an adverb meaning "harmfully," "wickedly," or "poorly." Your sentence appears to require *bad* (I *feel ill*), unless you mean that your sense of touch is impaired (I *feel poorly*).

PREPOSITIONS

OBJECTIVES

When you have completed the material in this chapter, you will be able to do the following:

- Use objective-case pronouns as objects of prepositions.
- Avoid using prepositions in place of verbs and adverbs.
- Use eight troublesome prepositions correctly.
- Omit unnecessary prepositions and retain necessary ones.
- Recognize those words and constructions requiring specific prepositions (idioms).

Prepositions are connecting words. They show the relationship of a noun or pronoun to another word in a sentence. This chapter reviews the use of objective-case pronouns following prepositions. It also focuses on common challenges that communicators have with troublesome prepositions. Finally, it presents many words in our language that require specific prepositions (idiomatic expressions) to sound "right."

BASIC USE OF PREPOSITIONS

Prepositions join nouns and pronouns to other words in a sentence. As the word itself suggests (*pre* meaning "before"), a preposition is a word in a position *before* its object (a noun or pronoun). Prepositions are used in phrases to show a relationship between the object of the preposition and another word in the sentence. In the following sentences notice that the preposition changes the relation of the object (*Denise Fuller*) to the verb (*talked*):

John Adams often talked *with* Denise Fuller.
John Adams often talked *about* Denise Fuller.
John Adams often talked *to* Denise Fuller.

In the following list, notice that prepositions may consist of one word or several.

about	below	from	on
according to	beside	in	on account of
after	between	in addition to	over
along with	but	in spite of	to
among	by	into	under
around	during	like	until
at	except	of	upon
before	for	off	with

SPOT THE BLOOPER

From a job applicant's cover letter: "I would be prepared to meet with you at your earliest convenience to discuss what I can do to your company."

SPOT THE BLOOPER

Photo caption in *The Tribune* [Greeley, Colorado]: "West's David Shaw hits the winning shot for he and Tom White."

SPOT THE BLOOPER

From *The New York Times:* " . . . reflecting on the hardships that pupils like she and Lakesha Perry face in Brownsville, Brooklyn . . . ."

Objective Case Following Prepositions

As you will recall from Chapter 3, pronouns that are objects of prepositions must be in the objective case.

> We received quotes *from him* and *her* for the network installation project.
> The disagreement is with the distributor, not *with you* and *me.*
> Give the account balances *to* Norma Jean Malterer and *him.*

Less frequently used prepositions are *like, between, except,* and *but* (meaning "except"). These prepositions may lead to confusion in determining pronoun case. Consider the following examples.

> Just *between you and me,* will the two companies merge? (Not *between you and I*)
> Volunteers *like Ann Pounds and him* are rare. (Not *like Ann Pounds and he*)
> Applications from everyone *but them* have arrived. (Not *but they*)

PREPOSITIONS THAT DESERVE SPECIAL ATTENTION

In even the most casual speech or writing, the following misuses of prepositions should be avoided.

■ *Of* for *have.*   The verb phrases *should have, could have,* and *would have* should never be written as *should of, could of,* and *would of.* The word *of* is a preposition and cannot be used in verb phrases.

> Juan *should have* called first. (Not *should of*)
> He *could have* given some advance notice. (Not *could of*)
> I *would have* covered for you if I had been available. (Not *would of*)

■ *Off* for *from.*   The preposition *from* should never be replaced by *off* or *off of.*

> Marsha borrowed a highlighter *from him.* (Not *off of*)
> Shannon said she got the correct answer *from* you. (Not *off* or *off of*)

■ *To* for *too.*   The preposition *to* means "in a direction toward." Do not use the word *to* in place of the adverb *too,* which means "additionally," "also," or "excessively." Remember also that the word *to* may be part of an infinitive construction.

> Dividends are not distributed *to* stockholders unless declared by the directors.
> No dividends were declared because profits were *too* small. (Meaning "excessively")
> Contributions of services will be accepted *too.* (Meaning "additionally" or "also")
> She is learning *to* program in HTML and Java. (*To* as part of the infinitive *to program*)

■ *Among, between.*   *Among* is usually used to speak of three or more persons or things; *between* is usually used for two.

> The disagreement was *between* him and his partner.
> Profits were distributed *among* the four partners.

■ *Beside, besides.*   *Beside* means "next to"; *besides* means "in addition to."

> The woman sitting *beside* me on the plane was Meg Whitman, the CEO of eBay.
> *Besides* an executive summary, you must write an introduction.

■ *Except.*   The preposition *except,* meaning "excluding" or "but," is sometimes confused with the verb *accept,* which means "to receive."

> Everyone *except* Craig Bjustrom was able to come.
> Did you *accept* the job offer from CitiGroup?

■ ***In, into, in to.*** *In* indicates a position or location. *Into* can mean several things, including the following: (1) entering something, (2) changing form, or (3) making contact. Some constructions may employ *in* as an adverb preceding an infinitive:

> The meeting will be held *in* the conference room. (Preposition *in* indicates location.)
> Come *into* my office to see my new monitor. (Preposition *into* indicates entering a location.)
> Their son is turning *into* a fine young man. (Preposition *into* indicates changing form.)
> I ran *into* Stan in the hall on my way to the board meeting. (Preposition *into* indicates making contact with someone.)
> They went *in* to see the manager. (Adverb *in* precedes infinitive *to see*.)

■ ***Like.*** The preposition *like* should be used to introduce a noun or pronoun. Do not use *like* to introduce a clause (a group of words with a subject and a predicate). To introduce clauses, use *as, as if,* or *as though*.

> She looks a lot *like* Heather Locklear. (Use *like* as a preposition to introduce the object, *Heather Locklear.*)
> She looks *as if* she is tired. (Use *as if* to introduce the clause *she is tired.*)
> *As* I said in my letter, I have experience in this field. (Do not use *like* to introduce the clause *I said in my letter.*)

NECESSARY AND UNNECESSARY PREPOSITIONS

Don't omit those prepositions necessary to clarify a relationship. Be particularly careful when two prepositions modify a single object.

> We have every desire *for* and anticipation *of* an early settlement. (Do not omit *for.*)
> What type *of* firewall would you like to install? (Do not omit *of.*)
> Don Foster is unsure *of* how to approach the problem. (Do not omit *of.*)
> Benefits are better for exempt employees than *for* nonexempt employees. (Do not omit *for.*)
> When did you graduate *from* college? (Do not omit *from.*)*

Omit unnecessary prepositions, particularly the word *of*.

> Leave the package *inside* the door. (Not *inside of*)
> Both Web sites are useful. (Not *of the Web sites*)
> All participants must sign a waiver. (Not *of the*)
> Where is the meeting? (Not *meeting at*)
> She could not help agreeing. (Rather than *help from*)
> Keep the paper near the printer. (Not *near to*)

IDIOMATIC USE OF PREPOSITIONS

Every language has idioms (word combinations that are peculiar to that language). These combinations have developed through usage and often cannot be explained rationally. A native speaker usually is unaware of idiom usage until a violation jars his or her ear, such as "He is capable *from* (rather than *of*) violence."

The following list shows words that require specific prepositions to denote precise meanings. This group is just a sampling of the large number of English

---

*See the third Hotline Query in this chapter (graduate from college).

idioms. Consult a dictionary when you are unsure of the correct preposition to use with a particular word.

acquainted with	Are you *acquainted with* our new manager?
addicted to	Jennifer is *addicted to* surfing the Web.
adept in	Are you *adept in* negotiation tactics?
adhere to	All employees must *adhere to* certain Internet-use policies.
agree on (mutual ideas)	Our team members *agree on* nearly everything.
agree to (a proposal)	Did they *agree to* reduced benefits?
agree with (a person)	I *agree with* you on this issue.
all of (when followed by a pronoun)	All *of us* contributed. (For efficiency omit *of* when *all* is followed by a noun, as *All members contributed.*)
angry at (a thing)	Many employees are *angry at* the change in vacation policy.
angry with (a person)	Are you *angry with* me for being late?
both of (when followed by a pronoun)	Both *of them* were hired. (For efficiency omit *of* when *both* is followed by a noun, as *Both candidates were hired.*)
buy from	You may *buy from* any one of several vendors.
capable of	We had no idea he was *capable of* such leadership.
comply with	We must *comply with* governmental regulations.
conform to	Your products do not *conform to* our specifications.
contrast with	The angles *contrast with* the curves in that logo design.
correspond to (match)	A company's success *corresponds to* its leadership.
correspond with (write)	We *correspond with* our clients regularly.
differ from (things)	How does your calling plan *differ from* Verizon's?
differ with (person)	I *differ with* you in small points only.
different from (not *than*)	This product is *different from* the one I ordered.
disagree with	Ron *disagrees with* me on just about everything.
expert in	Peter Churchill is an *expert in* the stock market.
guard against	We must *guard against* complacency.
identical with or to	Our floor plan is *identical with* (or *to*) yours.
independent of	Living alone, the young man was *independent of* his parents.
infer from	I *infer from* your comments that you are dissatisfied.
interest in	Jerry has a great *interest in* Web site design.
negligent of	Pat was *negligent of* the important duties of his position.
oblivious of or to	He is often *oblivious of* (or *to*) what goes on around him.
plan to (not *on*)	We *plan to* expand the marketing of our products.
prefer to	Do you *prefer to* work a four-day week?
reason with	We tried to *reason with* the unhappy customer.

SPOT THE BLOOPER

From the *Patriot-Ledger* [Quincy, Massachusetts]: "Clemens is able to come off the disabled list Sunday, but tests by Dr. Arthur Pappas led to the conclusion that Clemens' groin is still too weak to pitch in a game."

reconcile with (match)	Our expenditures must be *reconciled with* our budget.
reconcile to (accept)	Martin has never become *reconciled to* our decision to discontinue the product line.
responsible for	William is *responsible for* locking the building.
retroactive to (not *from*)	The salary increase is *retroactive to* the first of this year.
sensitive to	Our employer is especially *sensitive to* the needs of employees.
similar to	Your proposal is *similar to* mine.
standing in (not *on*) line	How long have you been *standing in* line?
talk to (tell something)	Gene will *talk to* us about the reorganization plans.
talk with (exchange remarks)	Let's *talk with* Teresa about our mutual goals.

You are now ready to complete the reinforcement exercises.

HOTLINE QUERIES

Q: I thought I knew the difference between *to* and *too*, but could you provide me with a quick review?

A: *To* may serve as a preposition (*I'm going to the store*), and it may also serve as part of an infinitive construction (*to sign his name*). The adverb *too* may be used to mean "also" (*Andrea will attend too*). In addition, the word *too* may be used to indicate "to an excessive extent" (*the letter is too long*).

Q: I was always taught that you should never end a sentence with a preposition. But sometimes following this rule sounds so stuffy and unnatural, such as saying *From where are you?* instead of *Where are you from?* Is it ever acceptable to end a sentence with a preposition?

A: In the past, language authorities warned against ending a sentence (or a clause) with a preposition. In formal writing today most careful authors continue to avoid terminal prepositions. In conversation and informal writing, however, terminal prepositions are acceptable.

Q: What's wrong with saying *Lisa graduated college last year?*

A: The preposition *from* must be inserted for syntactical fluency. Two constructions are permissible: *Lisa graduated from college* or *Lisa was graduated from college*. The first version is more popular; the second is preferred by traditional grammarians.

Q: Should *sometime* be one or two words in the following sentence? *Can you come over (some time) soon?*

A: In this sentence you should use the one-word form. *Sometime* means "an indefinite time" (*the convention is sometime in December*). The two-word combination means "a period of time" (*we have some time to spare*).

Q: I saw this printed recently: *Some of the personal functions that are being reviewed are job descriptions, job specifications, and job evaluation.* Is *personal* used correctly here?

A: Indeed not! The word *personal* means "private" or "individual" (*your personal letters are being forwarded to you*). The word *personnel* refers to employees (*all company personnel are cordially invited*). The sentence you quote requires *personnel*.

Q: Is there any difference between *proved* and *proven*?

A: As a past participle, the verb form *proved* is preferred (*he has proved his point*). However, the word *proven* is preferred as an adjective form (*that company has a proven record*). *Proven* is also commonly used in the expression *not proven*.

Q: We're writing a letter to our subscribers, and this sentence doesn't sound right to me: *Every one of our subscribers benefit . . . .*

A: As you probably suspected, the verb *benefit* does not agree with the subject *one*. The sentence should read as follows: *Every one of our subscribers benefits . . . .* Don't let intervening phrases obscure the true subject of a sentence.

Q: In my dictionary I found three ways to spell the same word: *lifestyle, life-style,* and *life style.* Which should I use?

A: The first spelling shown is usually the preferred one. In your dictionary a second acceptable form may be introduced by the word *also*. If two spellings appear side by side (*ax, axe*), they are equally acceptable.

Q: How should I write *industry wide*? It's not in my dictionary.

A: A word with the suffix *wide* is usually written solid: *industrywide, nationwide, countrywide, statewide, worldwide.*

Q: Can you tell me what sounds strange in this sentence and why? *The building looks like it was redesigned.*

A: The word *like* should not be used as a conjunction, as has been done in your sentence. Substitute *as if* (*the building looks as if it was redesigned*).

9

CONJUNCTIONS THAT JOIN EQUALS

OBJECTIVES   When you have completed the material in this chapter, you will be able to do the following:

- Distinguish between phrases and clauses
- Distinguish between simple and compound sentences.
- Punctuate compound sentences joined by the coordinating conjunctions *and, or, nor, but, so, for,* and *yet.*
- Punctuate compound sentences using conjunctive adverbs such as *therefore, however,* and *consequently.*
- Distinguish conjunctive adverbs from parenthetical adverbs.
- Recognize correlative conjunctions such as *either . . . or, not only . . . but also,* and *neither . . . nor.*
- Use a parallel construction in composing sentences with correlative conjunctions.

Conjunctions are connecting words. They may be separated into two major groups: those that join grammatically equal words or word groups and those that join grammatically unequal words or word groups. This chapter focuses on those conjunctions that join equals. Recognizing conjunctions and understanding their patterns of usage will, among other things, enable you to use commas and semicolons more appropriately.

COORDINATING CONJUNCTIONS

Coordinating conjunctions connect words, phrases, and clauses of equal grammatical value or rank. The most common coordinating conjunctions are *and, or, but,* and *nor.* Notice in these sentences that coordinating conjunctions join grammatically equal elements.

> The qualities I admire most are *honesty, integrity,* and *reliability.* (Here the word *and* joins equal words.)
> Open your mind *to new challenges* and *to new ideas.* (Here *and* joins equal phrases.)
> *Tiffany opens the mail,* but *Benjamin fills the orders.* (Here *but* joins equal clauses.)

Three other coordinating conjunctions should also be mentioned: *yet, for,* and *so.* The words *yet* and *for* may function as coordinating conjunctions, although they are infrequently used as such.

> We have only two hours left, *yet* we hope to finish.
> The weary traveler was gaunt and ill, *for* his journey had been long and arduous.

The word *so* is sometimes informally used as a coordinating conjunction. In more formal contexts the conjunctive adverbs *therefore* and *consequently* should be substituted for the conjunction *so*.

> INFORMAL: The plane leaves at 2:15, *so* you still have time to pack.
> FORMAL: The plane leaves at 2:15; *therefore,* you still have time to pack.

To avoid using *so* as a conjunction, try starting your sentence with *because* or *although*.

> INFORMAL: Cell phone calls in public can be intrusive, so they are banned in some places.
> IMPROVED: Because cell phone calls in public can be intrusive, they are banned in some places.

Phrases and Clauses

A group of related words without a subject and a verb is called a *phrase*. You are already familiar with verb phrases and prepositional phrases. It is not important that you be able to identify the other kinds of phrases (infinitive, gerund, participial), but it is very important that you be able to distinguish phrases from clauses.

The alarm was coming from another part of the building.
  phrase   phrase   phrase

A group of related words including a subject and a verb is a clause.

We interviewed three applicants, and we decided to hire Richard Royka.
        clause   clause

Karen is interested in a job in marketing, but she wants to travel also.
        clause   clause

                              phrase   phrase
Salaries begin at $45,000 annually, and they can reach over $80,000.
        clause   clause

Simple and Compound Sentences

A *simple sentence* has one independent clause, that is, a clause that can stand alone. A *compound sentence* has two or more independent clauses.

> Many people are concerned about identify theft. (Simple sentence.)
> Our Travel Department planned the sales trip, but some salespeople also made private excursions. (Compound sentence.)

Punctuating Compound Sentences

When coordinating conjunctions (*and, or, but,* and *nor*) join clauses in compound sentences, a comma generally precedes the conjunction. However, if the sentence is quite short (let's say, 12 or 13 total words), the comma may be omitted.

> We can ship the merchandise by air, *or* we can ship it by rail.
> Ship by UPS *or* ship by FedEx. (Clauses are too short to require a comma.)

Do not use commas when coordinating conjunctions join compound verbs, objects, or phrases.

The <u>bank</u> <u>will notify</u> you of each transfer, or <u>it</u> <u>will send</u> you a monthly statement. (Comma used because *or* joins two independent clauses.)

The <u>bank</u> <u>will notify</u> you of each transfer or <u>will send</u> you a monthly statement. (No comma needed because *or* joins the compound verbs of a single independent clause.)

<u>Our CEO</u> <u>said</u> that employees should not have to choose between working overtime *and* spending time with their families. (No comma needed because *and* joins the compound objects of a prepositional phrase.)

<u>Stockholders</u> <u>are expected</u> to attend the meeting *or* to send their proxies. (No comma needed because *or* joins two infinitive phrases.)

<u>Analyze</u> all your possible property risks, *and* <u>protect</u> yourself with insurance. (Comma needed to join two independent clauses; the subject of each clause is understood to be *you*.)

CONJUNCTIVE ADVERBS

Conjunctive adverbs may also be used to connect equal sentence elements. Because conjunctive adverbs are used to effect a transition from one thought to another, and because they may consist of more than one word, they have also been called *transitional expressions*. The most common conjunctive adverbs follow.

accordingly	in fact	on the other hand
consequently	in the meantime	that is
furthermore	moreover	then
hence	nevertheless	therefore
however	on the contrary	thus

In the following compound sentences, observe that conjunctive adverbs join clauses of equal grammatical value. Note that semicolons (NOT commas) are used before conjunctive adverbs that join independent clauses. Commas should immediately follow conjunctive adverbs of two or more syllables. Note also that the word following a semicolon is not capitalized—unless, of course, it is a proper noun.

Sarah did her best; *nevertheless,* she failed to pass the bar exam.

Some machines require separate outlets; *consequently,* new outlets were installed.

Equipment expenditures are great this quarter; *on the other hand,* new equipment will reduce labor costs.

The growing use of handheld phones in cars endangers safety; *thus* several communities are giving away free bumper stickers that say "Drive Now, Talk Later."

Competition in the telecommunications industry is intense; *hence* prices may decrease sharply.

Generally, no comma is used after one-syllable conjunctive adverbs such as *hence, thus,* and *then* (unless a strong pause is desired).

DISTINGUISHING CONJUNCTIVE ADVERBS FROM PARENTHETICAL ADVERBS

Many words that function as conjunctive adverbs may also serve as *parenthetical* (interrupting) *adverbs* that are employed to effect transition from one thought to another. Use semicolons *only* with conjunctive adverbs that join independent clauses. Use commas to set off parenthetical adverbs that interrupt the flow of a sentence.

The credit for our success, *however,* belongs to Rachel. (Adverb used parenthetically)

Robert deserves credit for our success; *however,* he will not accept it. (Conjunctive adverb used to join two clauses)

The Federal Reserve System, *moreover,* is a vital force in maintaining a sound banking system and a stable economy. (Adverb used parenthetically)

The Federal Reserve System is a vital force in maintaining a sound banking system; *moreover,* it is instrumental in creating a stable economy. (Conjunctive adverb used to join two clauses)

I am afraid, *on the other hand,* that we may lose money in the stock market. (Adverb used parenthetically)

I am afraid that we may lose money in the stock market; *on the other hand,* the current downturn in stock prices may be reversing. (Conjunctive adverb used to join two clauses)

CORRELATIVE CONJUNCTIONS

We have studied thus far two kinds of conjunctions used to join grammatically equal sentence elements: coordinating conjunctions (used to join equal words, phrases, and clauses) and conjunctive adverbs (used to join grammatically equal clauses in compound sentences). *Correlative conjunctions* form the third and final group of conjunctions that join grammatically equal sentence elements.

Correlative conjunctions are always paired: *both . . . and, not only . . . but (also), either . . . or,* and *neither . . . nor.* When greater emphasis is desired, these paired conjunctions are used instead of coordinating conjunctions.

Your best chances for advancement are in the marketing department *or* in the sales department.

Your best chances for advancement are *either* in the marketing department *or* in the sales department. (More emphatic)

In using correlative conjunctions, place them so that the words, phrases, or clauses being joined are parallel in construction.

NOT PARALLEL: *Either* Molly was flying to Dallas *or* to Houston.

PARALLEL: Molly was flying *either* to Dallas *or* to Houston.

NOT PARALLEL: She was *not only* talented, *but* she was *also* intelligent.

PARALLEL: She was *not only* talented *but also* intelligent.

NOT PARALLEL: I *neither* have the time *nor* the energy for this.

PARALLEL: I have *neither* the time *nor* the energy for this.

You are now ready to complete the reinforcement exercises.

Q: A friend of mine gets upset when I say something like, *I was so surprised by her remark.* She thinks I'm misusing *so.* Am I?

A: Your friend is right, if we're talking about formal expression. The intensifier *so* requires a clause to complete its meaning. For example, *I was so surprised by her remark that I immediately protested.* It's like waiting for the other shoe to drop when one hears *so* as a modifier without a qualifying clause. *He was so funny.* So funny that what? *He was so funny that he became a stand-up comedian.*

Q: Please help me decide which *maybe* to use in this sentence: *He said that he (maybe, may be) able to help us.*

A: Use the two-word *may be,* which is the verb form. *Maybe* is an adverb that means "perhaps" (*maybe she will call*).

Q: My English-teacher aunt says that I should say, *My cell phone is not <u>so</u> clear as yours* instead of *My cell phone is not <u>as</u> clear as yours.* Is she right?

A: As a matter of style in negative comparisons, some people prefer to use *not so . . . as.* However, it is just as acceptable to say *not as . . . as* (for example, *price is not as* (or *so*) *important as location*).

Q: At the end of a printed line, is it acceptable to type part of an individual's name on one line and carry the rest to the next line?

A: Full names may be divided between the first and last names or after the middle initial. For example, you could type *John R.* on one line and *Williamson* on the next line. Do not, however, separate a short title and a surname (such as *Mr./Williamson*), and do not divide a name (such as *William/son*). By the way, many computer programs make unacceptable line-ending decisions. Be sure to inspect your copy, either on the screen or on the printout, so that you can correct poor hyphenation and unacceptable word separations.

Q: What should the verb in this sentence be? *There (has, have) to be good reasons . . .*

A: Use the plural verb *have,* which agrees with the subject *reasons.* In sentences that begin with the word *there,* look for the subject after the verb.

Q: Does *Ms.* have a period after it? Should I use this title for all women in business today?

A: *Ms.* is probably a blend of *Miss* and *Mrs.* It is written with a period following it. Some women in business prefer to use *Ms.,* presumably because it is a title equal to *Mr.* Neither title reveals one's marital status. Many other women, however, prefer to use *Miss* or *Mrs.* as a title. It's always wise, if possible, to determine the preference of the individual.

HOTLINE QUERIES

Q: I just typed this sentence: *He was given a new title in lieu of a salary increase.* I went to my dictionary to check the spelling of *in lieu of,* but I can't find it. How is it spelled and what does it mean?

A: The listing in the dictionary is under *lieu,* and it means "instead of." Many authorities today are recommending that such phrases be avoided. It's easier and clearer to say "instead of."

Q: Can you help me with the words *averse* and *adverse?* I've never been able to straighten them out in my mind.

A: *Averse* is an adjective meaning "disinclined" and generally is used with the preposition *to* (*the little boy was averse to bathing; she is averse to statistical typing*). *Adverse* is also an adjective, but it means "hostile" or "unfavorable" (*adverse economic conditions halted the company's growth; the picnic was postponed because of adverse weather conditions*). In distinguishing between these two very similar words, it might help you to

know that the word *averse* is usually used to describe animate (living) objects.

Q: What should I write: *You are our No. 1 account,* or *You are our number one account?* Should anything be hyphenated?

A: Either is correct, but we prefer *No. 1* because it is more easily recognizable. No hyphen is required.

Q: My colleague says that this sentence is correct: *Please complete this survey regarding your satisfaction at our dealership, return it in the enclosed addressed envelope.* I think something is wrong, but I'm not sure what.

A: You're right. This sentence has two independent clauses, and some writers attempt to join them with a comma. But this construction produces a comma splice. You can correct the problem by adding *and* between the clauses, starting a new sentence, or using a semicolon between the clauses.

10

CONJUNCTIONS THAT JOIN UNEQUALS

OBJECTIVES

When you have completed the material in this chapter,.you will be able to do the following:

- Distinguish between dependent clauses and independent clauses.
- Understand how relative pronouns can be used as conjunctions.
- Punctuate introductory and terminal dependent clauses.
- Punctuate parenthetical, essential, and nonessential dependent clauses.
- Recognize simple, compound, complex, and compound-complex sentences.
- Convert simple sentences into a variety of more complex patterns.

In Chapter 9 you learned about conjunctions that join equal sentence elements such as words, phrases, and clauses. These equal sentence parts were joined by coordinating conjunctions (*and, or, nor, but*), conjunctive adverbs (such as *therefore, however, consequently*), and correlative conjunctions (such as *either . . . or*). Now let's look at a special group of conjunctions that join unequal sentence parts.

SUBORDINATING CONJUNCTIONS

To join unequal sentence elements, such as independent and dependent clauses, use *subordinating conjunctions*. A list of the most common subordinating conjunctions follows.

after	because	provided	until
although	before	since	when
as	even though	so that	where
as if	if	that	whether
as though	in order that	unless	while

You should become familiar with this list of conjunctions, but do not feel that you must at all times be able to recall every subordinating conjunction. Generally, you can recognize a subordinating conjunction by the way it limits, or subordinates, the clause it introduces. In the clause *because he always paid with cash,* the subordinating conjunction *because* limits the meaning of the clause it introduces. The clause is incomplete and could not stand alone as a sentence.

INDEPENDENT AND DEPENDENT CLAUSES

Main clauses that can stand alone are said to be *independent*. They have subjects and verbs and make sense by themselves.

Business writing should be concise. (One main clause)

Business writing should be concise, and it should be clear as well. (Two main clauses)

Judy Foster writes many e-mail memos, but Robert Eustes writes more letters. (Two main clauses)

Clauses that cannot stand alone are said to be *dependent*. They have subjects and verbs, but they depend on other clauses for the completion of their meaning. Dependent clauses are often introduced by subordinating conjunctions. Dependent clauses may precede or follow independent clauses.

STUDY TIP▼

Dependent clauses should never be written or punctuated as if they were complete sentences.

Dependent clause	Independent clause

When Leonard Goodleman wants a quick reply, he sends an e-mail message.

Dependent clause	Independent clause

If you have any questions, please call me at Extension 2306.

Independent clause	Dependent clause

Please call me at Extension 2306 if you have any questions.

SPOT THE BLOOPER

From a set of bylaws: "Each condominium unit may have a reasonable number of household pets. Which at the desecration of the Association do not create a nuisance to other owners." (Can you spot two errors?)

RELATIVE PRONOUNS

The relative pronouns *who, whom, whose, which,* and *that* actually function as conjunctions when they introduce dependent clauses. *Who* is used to refer to persons. It may introduce essential or nonessential clauses. *That* refers to animals or things and should be used to introduce essential clauses. *Which* refers to animals or things and introduces nonessential clauses.

The tricky part is deciding whether a clause is essential or nonessential. Nonessential clauses contain information that the reader does not need to know; the main clause is understandable without this extra information. In some cases, only the writer knows whether a clause is intended to be essential or nonessential. If it is nonessential, it should be set off from the rest of the sentence by commas. You'll learn more about punctuating these sentences shortly.

Anyone *who* (not *that*) has a computer can create a Web site. (The relative pronoun *who* refers to a person, and it introduces an essential clause.)

A company *that* (not *who* or *which*) values its employees is likely to succeed. (The relative pronoun *that* introduces an essential clause.)

Software giant Microsoft, *which* is headquartered in Redmond, has many other offices in the state of Washington. (The relative pronoun *which* introduces a nonessential clause and is set off by commas.)

Microsoft is the company *that* (not *which*) is headquartered in Redmond. (The relative pronoun *that* introduces an essential clause and requires no commas.)

Allan Lacayo, *who* has excellent recommendations, is applying for a position in our department. (The relative pronoun *who* introduces a nonessential clause and is set off by commas.)

PUNCTUATION OF SENTENCES WITH DEPENDENT CLAUSES

Business writers are especially concerned with clarity and accuracy. A misplaced or omitted punctuation mark can confuse a reader by altering the meaning of a sentence. The following guidelines for using commas help ensure clarity and consistency in writing. Some professional writers, however, take liberties with accepted conventions of punctuation, particularly in regard to comma usage. These experienced writers may omit a comma when they feel that such an omission will not affect the reader's understanding of a sentence. Beginning writers, though, are well advised to first develop skill in punctuating sentences by following traditional guidelines.

Introductory Dependent Clauses

Use a comma after a dependent (subordinate) clause that precedes an independent clause.

> *Even though* Philo Farnsworth invented the television in 1927, he was never able to personally introduce it to consumers.
> *Because* President Franklin Roosevelt passed a series of securities laws in the 1930s, he helped create the Securities and Exchange Commission (SEC) to enforce them.
> *When* he gets here, we can start the meeting.

Use a comma after an introductory dependent clause even though the subject and verb may not be stated.

> *As* [it is] expected, the opening is delayed.
> *If* [it is] possible, ship our order today.
> *When* [they are] printed, your brochures will be distributed.

Terminal Dependent Clauses

Generally, a dependent clause introduced by a subordinating conjunction does not require a comma when the dependent clause falls at the end of a sentence.

> We must finish the research *before* we write the report.
> They cannot leave *until* the manager returns.
> Be prepared to distribute brochures and annual reports *when* the clients arrive.

If, however, the dependent clause at the end of a sentence interrupts the flow of the sentence and sounds as if it were an afterthought, a comma should be used.

> I am sure I paid the bill, *although* I cannot find my receipt. (Dependent clause adds unnecessary information.)
> We will ship the goods within the week, *if* that is satisfactory with you. (Dependent clause adds unnecessary information.)

Parenthetical Clauses

Within a sentence, dependent clauses that interrupt the flow of a sentence and are unnecessary for the grammatical completeness of the sentence are set off by commas.

> The motion, *unless* you want further discussion, will be tabled until our next meeting.
> At our next meeting, *provided* we have a quorum, the motion will be reconsidered.

Relative Clauses

You learned earlier that the relative pronouns *who, which,* and *that* can function as conjunctions when they introduce dependent clauses. The relative pronoun *who* may introduce essential (restrictive) or nonessential (nonrestrictive) clauses. The relative pronoun *that* is used to introduce essential (restrictive) clauses. And the relative pronoun *which* is used to introduce nonessential (restrictive) clauses.

SPOT THE BLOOPER

From classified ads in local newspapers: "LAWNMORE SHOP" and a house for sale with "walking closets."

STUDY TIP

Careful writers use the word *that* for essential clauses and the word *which* for nonessential clauses. Dependent clauses introduced by *which* require commas.

Remember that an *essential clause* is needed to identify the noun to which it refers; therefore, no commas should separate this clause from its antecedent.

> Any employee *who wants an August vacation* must apply soon. (The dependent clause is essential because it is needed to identify which employees must apply soon.)
>
> Network passwords *that were issued last month* must be changed by Friday. (The dependent clause is essential because it is needed to identify which network passwords be changed.)

A *nonessential clause* supplies additional information that is not needed to identify its antecedent; therefore, commas are used to separate the nonessential information from the rest of the sentence. Notice that *two* commas are used to set off internal nonessential dependent clauses.

> James Awbrey, *who wants an August vacation,* must apply soon. (The antecedent of the dependent clause, James Awbrey, is clearly identified.)
>
> Network passwords for all support staff, *which were issued last month,* must be changed by Friday. (The antecedent of the dependent clause is clearly identified.)

Punctuation Review

The following three common sentence patterns are very important for you to study and understand. Notice particularly how they are punctuated.

Independent clause (,) + { and / or / nor / but } + Independent clause. (Comma used when a coordinating conjunction joins independent clauses.)

Independent clause (;) + { therefore, / consequently, / however, / nevertheless, } + Independent clause. (Semicolon used when a conjunctive adverb joins independent clauses.)

{ Since / If / As / When } Dependent clause (,) + Independent clause. (Comma used after a dependent clause introduced by a subordinate conjunction.)

SENTENCE VARIETY

To make messages more interesting, good writers strive for variety in sentence structure. Notice the monotony and choppiness of a paragraph made up entirely of simple sentences:

> Rena Pocrass founded a dessert business in 1995. She specialized in molded containers made of French chocolate. Her 350 designs were unique. She copyrighted them. Another chocolatier copied her spiral chocolate seashell. Rena sued. She won.

Compare the following version of this paragraph, which uses dependent clauses and other structures to achieve greater sentence variety:

> Rena Pocrass, *who* founded a dessert business in 1995, specialized in molded containers made of French chocolate. *Because* her 350 designs were

unique, she copyrighted them. *When* another chocolatier copied her spiral chocolate seashell, Rena sued and won.

Recognizing the kinds of sentence structures available to writers and speakers is an important step in achieving effective expression. Let's review the three kinds of sentence structures that you have been studying and include a fourth category as well.

KIND OF SENTENCE	MINIMUM REQUIREMENT	EXAMPLE
Simple	One independent clause	Rena Pocrass founded a dessert business in 1995.
Compound	Two independent clauses	Rena founded a dessert business in 1995, and she specialized in molded containers of French chocolate.
Complex	One independent clause and one dependent clause	Rena Pocrass, who founded a dessert business in 1995, specialized in molded containers of French chocolate.
Compound-complex	Two independent clauses and one dependent clause	Rena's chocolate designs were copyrighted; therefore, when another chocolatier copied one, she sued and won.

Developing the ability to use a variety of sentence structures to facilitate effective communication takes practice and writing experience.

You are now ready to complete the reinforcement exercises.

HOTLINE QUERIES

Q: **I don't think I'll ever be able to know the difference between *that* and *which*. Any advice for keeping them straight?**

A: The problem usually is the substitution of *which* for *that.* Whenever you're tempted to use *which*, remember that it requires a comma. Think *which + comma.* If the sentence doesn't sound right with a comma, then you know you need *that.* One eminent language specialist, William Strunk, advised careful writers to go *which*-hunting and remove all defining *whiches.* Examples: *The contract that we sent in June was just returned* (defines which one).

The Wilson contract, which we sent in June, was just returned (adds a fact about the only contract in question).

Q: I don't seem to be able to hear the difference between *than* and *then.* Can you explain it to me?

A: The conjunction *than* is used to make comparisons (*your watch is more accurate than mine*). The adverb *then* means "at that time" (*we must complete this task; then we will take our break*) or "as a consequence" (*if all the angles of the triangle are equal, then it must be equilateral as well*).

Q: Can the word *that* be omitted from sentences? For example, *She said [that] she would come.*

A: The relative pronoun *that* is frequently omitted in conversation and casual writing. For absolute clarity, however, skilled writers include it.

Q: Is there some rule about putting periods in organization names that are abbreviated? For example, does *IBM* have periods?

A: When the names of well-known business, educational, governmental, labor, and other organizations or agencies are abbreviated, periods are normally not used to separate the letters. Thus, no periods would appear in IBM, ITT, UCLA, AFL-CIO, YWCA, or AMA.

The names of radio and television stations and networks are also written without periods: Station WJR, KNX-FM, PBS, WABC-TV. Geographical abbreviations, however, generally do require periods: U.S.A., U.S.S.R., S.A. The two-letter state abbreviations recommended by the U.S. Postal Service require no periods: NY, OH, CA, MI, NJ, OR, MA, and so on.

Q: In this sentence which word should I use? *Your order will be sent to you in the (later or latter) part of the week.*

A: Use *latter.* The word *latter* designates the second of two persons or things. In addition, *latter* can be used to mean "further advanced in time or sequence," or *latter* can be used to contrast with *former.* In your sentence, the *latter* part of the week contrasts with the *former* part of the week.

Q: We're having a sale on *nonChristmas* items. Should a hyphen follow *non?* In my dictionary the prefix *non* is not hyphenated when it is joined to other words.

A: A hyphen is not used when a prefix is joined to most words: *nonessential, prewar, unwelcome, anticlimax.* A hyphen is used, however, when a prefix is joined to a proper (capitalized) noun: *non-Christmas, pre-Columbian, un-Christian, anti-American.*

11

COMMAS

When you have completed the material in this chapter, you will be able to do the following:

- Correctly place commas in series and direct address.
- Use commas correctly in punctuating dates, time zones, addresses, geographical items, and appositives.
- Place commas correctly in punctuating independent adjectives, parenthetical expressions, prepositional phrases, and verbal phrases.
- Use commas correctly in punctuating independent, introductory, terminal, and nonessential clauses.
- Use commas correctly in punctuating degrees, abbreviations, and numerals.
- Use commas to indicate omitted words, contrasting statements, clarity, and short quotations.

DID YOU KNOW?

Some writers in other languages envy English. Our systematic use of commas and other punctuation makes it easy to signal pauses, to emphasize ideas, and to enhance readability.

When you talk with a colleague, you are probably unaware of the "invisible" commas, periods, and other punctuation marks that you are using. In conversation your pauses and voice inflections punctuate your thoughts and clarify your meaning. In writing, however, you must use a conventional set of symbols, punctuation marks, to help your reader understand your meaning.

Over the years we have gradually developed a standardized pattern of usage for all punctuation marks. This usage has been codified (set down) in rules that are observed by writers who wish to make their writing as precise as possible. As noted earlier, some professional writers may deviate from conventional punctuation practices. In addition, some organizations, particularly newspapers and publishing houses, maintain their own style manuals to establish a consistent "in-house" style.

The punctuation guidelines presented in this book represent a consensus of punctuation styles that are acceptable in business writing. Following these guidelines will enable you to write with clarity, consistency, and accuracy.

SPOT THE BLOOPER

Poster for a university departmental event: "Door prizes will include lab equipment, books written by members of the biology department and a fruitcake."

GUIDELINES FOR USING COMMAS

The most used and misused punctuation mark, the comma, indicates a pause in the flow of a sentence. *Not all sentence pauses, however, require commas.* It is important for you to learn the standard rules for the use of commas so that you will not be tempted to clutter your sentences with needless, distracting commas. Here are the guidelines for comma usage.

Series

Commas are used to separate three or more equally ranked (coordinate) elements (words, phrases, or short clauses) in a series. A comma before the conjunction ensures separation of the last two items. No commas are used when conjunctions join all the items in a series.

> Only in June, July, and August are discounts offered. (Series of words. Notice that a comma precedes *and,* but no comma follows the last item, *August.*)
>
> Kevin Twohy conducted the research, organized the data, and wrote the first draft of the engineering report. (Series of phrases)
>
> Denise Morita is the owner, Chuck Risby is the marketing manager, and Cheryl Summers is the executive assistant. (Series of clauses)
>
> We need wireless access to e-mail and Web sites and the home office. (No commas needed when conjunctions are repeated.)

Direct Address

Words and phrases of direct address are set off with commas.

> I do believe, *Daphne,* that you have outdone yourself.
>
> I respectfully request, *sir,* that I be transferred.

Dates and Time Zones

When dates contain more than one element, the second and succeeding elements are normally set off by commas. Also use commas to set off time zones used with clock times. Study the following illustrations.

■ *Dates*

> On January 8 we opened for business. (No comma needed for one element.)
>
> On January 8, 2004, we opened for business. (Two commas set off second element.)
>
> On Monday, January 8, 2004, we opened for business. (Commas set off second and third elements.)
>
> In June, 2004, the reorganization was effected. (Commas set off second element.)
>
> **Note:** In June 2004 the reorganization was effected. (This alternate style is also acceptable.)

■ *Time Zones*

> Our flight leaves Newark at 8:05 a.m., EST, and arrives in Salt Lake City at 1:35 p.m., MST.
>
> He placed his online bid at 6:38 p.m., PST, which was two minutes before the auction closed.

Addresses and Geographical Items

When addresses and geographical items contain more than one element, the second and succeeding elements are normally set off by commas. Study the following illustrations.

■ *Addresses*

> Please send the application to Ms. Barbara Briggs, 1913 Piazza Court, Baton Rouge, Louisiana 70817, by Friday. (Commas are used between all elements except the state and zip code, which are in this special instance to be considered a single unit.)

■ *Geographical items*

> He moved from Nashville, Tennessee, to Chicago, Illinois. (Two commas set off the state unless it appears at the end of the sentence.)
> Her business will take her to Paris, France, and Brussels, Belgium, next month.

Appositives

You will recall that appositives rename or explain preceding nouns or pronouns. An appositive that provides information not essential to the identification of its antecedent should be set off by commas.

> Nancy Deason, *the Sun Microsystems sales representative,* is here. (The appositive adds nonessential information; commas set it off.)
> The sales representative *Nancy Deason* is here to see you. (The appositive is needed to identify which sales representative has arrived; therefore, no commas are used.)

One-word appositives do not require commas.

> My supervisor *Doug* sometimes uses my computer.

Independent Adjectives

Separate two or more adjectives that equally modify a noun (see Chapter 7).

> Online customers can conduct *secure, real-time* banking transactions.
> We're looking for an *industrious, ambitious* person to hire.

Parenthetical Expressions

Parenthetical words, phrases, and clauses may be used to create transitions between thoughts. These expressions interrupt the flow of a sentence and are unessential to its grammatical completeness. These commonly used expressions, some of which are listed here, are considered nonessential because they do not answer specifically questions such as *when? where? why?* or *how?* Set off these expressions with commas.

accordingly	hence	namely
after all	however	needless to say
all things considered	in addition	nevertheless
as a matter of fact	incidentally	no doubt
as a result	in conclusion	of course
as a rule	in fact	on the contrary
at any rate	in general	on the other hand
at the same time	in my opinion	otherwise
by the way	in other words	that is
consequently	in the first place	therefore
finally	in the meantime	under the circumstances
for example	likewise	unfortunately
furthermore	moreover	without a doubt

In addition, your computer skills are excellent. (At beginning of sentence)
This report is not, *however,* one that must be classified. (Inside sentence)
You have checked with other suppliers, *no doubt.* (At end of sentence)

These expressions are set off by commas only when they are used parenthetically and actually interrupt the flow of a sentence.

> *However* the vote goes, we will abide by the result. (No comma needed after *however.*)
>
> We have *no doubt* that our Web site must be redesigned. (No commas needed to set off *no doubt.*)

STUDY TIP

Phrases are essential (no commas) when they answer the questions *when? where? why?* or *how?*

Prepositional Phrases

Don't confuse short introductory essential prepositional phrases for parenthetical expressions. Notice that the following phrases are essential and, therefore, require no commas.

> *In the spring* more rental units become available. (No comma is needed because the short prepositional phrase answers the question *when?*)
>
> *At our Allentown branch* we will hire additional personnel. (No comma is needed because the short prepositional phrase answers the question *where?*)
>
> *For this reason* we must be at the meeting. (No comma is needed because the short prepositional phrase answers the question *why?*)
>
> *With your help* our production team can meet its goal. (No comma is needed because the short prepositional phrase answers the question *how?*)

One or more introductory prepositional phrases totaling five or more words should be followed by a comma.

> *On the third Tuesday of each month,* we hold a task force meeting.
>
> *In a company of this size,* standards and procedures are necessary.

Introductory prepositional phrases of fewer than five words require NO commas.

> *In 2005* we expect to expand our operations to Taiwan.
>
> *In this case* I believe we can waive the filing fee.

Prepositional phrases in other positions do not require commas when they are essential and do not interrupt the flow of the sentence.

> We have installed *in our Chicago office* a centralized telecommunications system. (No commas are needed around the prepositional phrase because it answers the question *where?* and does not interrupt the flow of the sentence.)
>
> You may *at your convenience* stop by to pick up your check. (No commas are needed because the prepositional phrase answers the question *when?* and does not interrupt the flow of the sentence.)

Introductory Verbal Phrases

Verbal phrases (see Chapter 6) that precede main clauses should be followed by commas.

> *To qualify for the position,* you must have two years' experience.
>
> *Working overtime,* we completed the project by the end of the week.

Independent Clauses

When a coordinating conjunction (see Chapter 9) joins independent clauses, use a comma before the coordinating conjunction, unless the clauses are very short (fewer than six words in each clause).

In Japan the wireless Internet has become wildly successful, and companies are pushing for even more sophisticated services.

Matthew uses his cell phone and Jan prefers her PDA. (No comma is needed since both clauses are short.)

STUDY TIP

The comma after an introductory clause is probably the most frequently missed comma in student writing. Be sure to insert a comma after a clause beginning with a subordinating conjunction such as *if, when, as,* or *since* (see Chapter 10).

Introductory Clauses

Dependent clauses that precede independent clauses are followed by commas.

> *When you have finished,* please return the style manual.
> *If you need help,* please call me in the afternoon.
> *Since we rely on e-mail,* we have cut back on voice mail.

Terminal Dependent Clauses

Whether to use a comma to separate a dependent clause at the end of a sentence depends on whether the added information is essential. Generally, terminal clauses add information that answers questions such as *when? why?* and *how?* Such information is essential; thus no comma is necessary. Only when a terminal clause adds unnecessary information should a comma be used.

> Please return the style manual *when you have finished.* (No comma is needed because the terminal clause provides essential information and answers the question *when?*)
> Just call me in the afternoon *if you need help.* (No comma is needed because the terminal clause provides essential information and answers the question *why?*)
> I plan to leave at 3:30, *although I could stay if you need me.* (A comma is needed because the terminal clause provides additional unnecessary information.)

SPOT THE BLOOPER

From a sports column in *The Atlanta Journal-Constitution:* "[The teams] were tied, thanks to Smith, who had spent Saturday night at the hospital witnessing the birth of his daughter, who on Sunday had lofted a pinch-hit home run."

Nonessential Clauses

Use commas to set off clauses that are used parenthetically or that supply information unneeded for the grammatical completeness of a sentence.

> An increase in employee benefits, *as you can well understand,* must be postponed until profits improve. (Commas are needed because the italicized clause adds unnecessary information.)
> We received a reply from Senator Diane Feinstein, *who will be visiting our firm next week.* (Commas are necessary because the italicized clause adds unnecessary information.)
> The culprit behind the spam, which advertised everything from cable descramblers to herbal remedies, was finally apprehended. (Commas are necessary because the italicized clause adds unneeded information. The relative pronoun *which* is a clue that the clause is unnecessary.)

Do NOT use commas to set off clauses that contain essential information.

> An executive assistant *who is preparing proposals* certainly needs an up-to-date reference manual. (No commas are necessary because the italicized clause is essential; it tells what executive assistant needs an up-to-date reference manual.)

SPOT THE BLOOPER

From *The Pacifica Tribune* [Pacifica, California]: "The land was eventually sold to Andy Oddstad who built homes and also became the site of Linda Mar Shopping Center."

Degrees and Abbreviations

Except for *Jr.* and *Sr.,* degrees, personal titles, and professional designations following individuals' names are set off by commas.

James O'Keefe Jr. is frequently confused with James O'Keefe Sr.

Cynthia Heilesen, M.D., has a flourishing practice in Tempe, Arizona.

Yukie Tokuyama, Ph.D., discussed degree requirements with the college president.

We have retained John Grant, Esq., to represent us.

The abbreviations *Inc.* and *Ltd.* are set off by commas if the company's legal name includes the commas.

Printrak International, Inc., helps law enforcement agencies ensure safety and security by integrating cross-platform applications. (Company's legal name includes comma.)

Global Industries Ltd. provides offshore construction in the Gulf of Mexico and West Africa. (Legal name does not include comma before *Inc.*)

Numerals

Unrelated figures appearing side by side should be separated by commas.

By 2008, 2.3 billion subscribers will be using wireless devices worldwide.

Numbers of more than three digits require commas.

1,760   47,950   6,500,000

However, calendar years and zip codes are written without commas within the numerals.

CALENDAR YEARS:	1776	1968	2010
ZIP CODES:	02116	45327	90265

Telephone numbers, house numbers, decimals, page numbers, serial numbers, and contract numbers are also written without commas within the numerals.

TELEPHONE NUMBER:	(415) 937-5594
HOUSE NUMBER:	5411 Redfield Circle
DECIMAL NUMBER:	.98651, .0050
PAGE NUMBER:	Page 356
SERIAL NUMBER:	36-5710-1693285763
CONTRACT NUMBER:	NO. 359063420

Omitted Words

A comma is used to show the omission of words that are understood.

Last summer we hired 12 interns; this summer, only 3 interns. (Comma shows omission of *we hired* after *summer.*)

Contrasting Statements

Commas are used to set off contrasting or opposing expressions. These expressions are often introduced by such words as *not, never, but,* and *yet.*

We chose Tommaso's, not Steps of Rome, to cater our reception. (Two commas set off the contrasting statement that appears in the middle of a sentence.)

Our earnings this year have been lower, yet quite adequate. (One comma sets off the contrasting statement that appears at the end of a sentence.)

The more he protests, the less we believe. (One comma sets off the contrasting statement that appears at the end of a sentence.)

Clarity

Commas are used to separate words repeated for emphasis and words that may be misread if not separated.

> James Trick said it was a very, very complex contract.
> Whoever goes, goes at his or her own expense.
> No matter what, you know you have our support.
> In business, time is money.

Short Quotations

A comma is used to separate a short quotation from the rest of a sentence. If the quotation is divided into two parts, two commas are used.

> Christine Schneider said, "The first product to use a bar code was Wrigley's gum."
> "The first product to use a bar code," said Christine Schneider, "was Wrigley's gum."

You are now ready to complete the reinforcement exercises.

STUDY TIP ▼

Here's a good rule to follow in relation to the comma: *When in doubt, leave it out!*

HOTLINE QUERIES

Q: I remember when company names with "Inc." and "Ltd." always had commas around these abbreviations. Has this changed?

A: Today's practice is to use commas only if the official company name includes the commas. For example, the following company names are written without commas: Phizer Inc., Canon Inc., Caterpillar Inc. However, other companies include the commas: Motorola, Inc.; Novell, Inc.; Macromedia, Inc.; Castle Rock Entertainment, Inc. One way to check on the official name is to search for the company's Web site and look at it there.

Q: My boss always leaves out the comma before the word *and* when it precedes the final word in a series of words. Should the comma be used?

A: Although some writers omit that comma, present practice favors its use so that the last two items in the series cannot be misread as one item. For example, *The departments participating are Engineering, Accounting, Personnel, and Human Resources.* Without that final comma, the last two items might be confused as one item.

Q: Should I use a comma after the year in this sentence? *In 2004 we began operations.*

A: No. Commas are not required after short introductory prepositional phrases unless confusion might result without them. If two numbers, for example, appear consecutively, a comma would be necessary to prevent confusion: *In 2004, 156 companies used our services.*

Q: Are these three words interchangeable: *assure, ensure,* and *insure?*

A: Good question! Although all three words mean "to make secure or certain," they are not interchangeable. *Assure* refers to persons and may suggest setting someone's mind at rest *(let me assure you that we are making every effort to locate it).* *Ensure* and *insure* both mean "to make secure from loss," but only *insure* is now used in the sense of protecting or indemnifying

against loss *(the building and its contents are insured).*

Q: It seems to me that the word *explanation* should be spelled as *explain* is spelled. Isn't this unusual?

A: Many words derived from root words change their grammatical form and spelling. Consider these: *maintain, maintenance; repeat, repetition; despair, desperate, desperation; pronounce, pronunciation; disaster, disastrous.*

Q: Is *appraise* used correctly in this sentence? *We will appraise stockholders of the potential loss.*

A: No. Your sentence requires *apprise,* which means "to inform or notify." The word *appraise* means "to estimate" *(he will appraise your home before you set its selling price).*

Q: Which word is correct in this sentence? *The officer (cited, sited, sighted) me for speeding.*

A: Your sentence requires *cited,* which means "to summon" or "to quote." *Site* means "a location," as in *a building site* or a *Web site. Sight* means "a view" or "to take aim," as in *the building was in sight.*

12

SEMICOLONS AND COLONS

OBJECTIVES

When you have completed the material in this chapter, you will be able to do the following:

- Use semicolons correctly in punctuating compound sentences.
- Use semicolons when necessary to separate items in a series.
- Distinguish between the use of commas and semicolons preceding expressions such as *namely, that is,* and *for instance.*
- Understand why semicolons are sometimes necessary to separate independent clauses joined by *and, or, nor,* or *but.*
- Distinguish between the proper and improper use of colons to introduce listed items.
- Correctly use colons to introduce quotations and explanatory sentences.
- Use colons appropriately and be able to capitalize words following colons when necessary.

Skilled writers use semicolons and colons to signal readers about the ideas that will follow. Semicolons tell readers that two closely related ideas should be thought of together. The semicolon is a stronger punctuation mark than a comma, which signifies a pause; but the semicolon is not as strong as a period, which signifies a complete stop. Understanding the use of semicolons will help you avoid fundamental writing errors, such as the *comma splice* and the *run-on sentence.* This chapter presents guidelines for using semicolons and colons effectively and correctly.

GUIDELINES FOR USING SEMICOLONS

The most basic use of the semicolon occurs in compound sentences. Many business communicators use a comma when they should be using a semicolon. Study the following examples to make sure you don't make this error. You will also learn other ways to use the semicolon in your writing.

STUDY TIP

Remember that a comma is used only after a two-syllable conjunctive adverb. And don't capitalize the word following a semicolon unless it's a proper noun.

Independent Clauses Separated by Conjunctive Adverbs

Semicolons are used primarily when two independent clauses are separated by a conjunctive adverb or a transitional expression. You studied this basic semicolon use in Chapter 9. Here are some review examples.

> Courtney wanted to improve her career opportunities; *consequently,* she went back to school. (A semicolon separates two independent clauses joined by the conjunctive adverb *consequently.*)

Companies make no profits until they recover costs; *therefore,* most companies use a cost approach in pricing. (A semicolon separates two independent clauses joined by the conjunctive adverb *therefore.*)

Barbara Sawyer worked for the university for over 20 years; *thus* she had witnessed many changes. (A semicolon separates two independent clauses joined by the conjunctive adverb *thus.*)

Independent Clauses Without a Coordinating Conjunction or a Conjunctive Adverb

Two or more closely related independent clauses not separated by a conjunctive adverb or a coordinating conjunction (*and, or, nor, but*) require a semicolon.

Sales meetings during prosperous times were lavish productions that focused on entertainment; meetings today focus on training and motivation.

Not all job openings are found in classified ads or in job databases; the "hidden" job market accounts for as many as two thirds of all available positions.

Occasionally, skillful writers use a comma to separate short, closely related independent clauses. As a business writer, however, you'll never be wrong if you use a semicolon to separate two independent clauses.

ACCEPTABLE: Sue provided the business experience, Dan provided the capital.

BETTER: Sue provided the business experience; Dan provided the capital.

Series Containing Internal Commas or Complete Thoughts

Semicolons are used to separate items in a series when one or more of the items contain internal commas.

Our branches in Austin, Texas; San Jose, California; and São Paulo, Brazil, are showing significant profits.

Attending the conference were Merv Maruyama, executive vice president, Cabrillo Industries; Carla Chambers, president, Santa Rosa Software; and Sharon Forester, program director, Club Mediterranean.

Semicolons are used to separate three or more serial independent clauses.

The first step consists of surveying all available information related to the company objective so that an understanding of all problems can be reached; the second step involves interviewing consumers, wholesalers, and retailers; and the third step consists of developing a research design in which the actual methods and procedures to be used are indicated.

A series of short independent clauses, however, may be separated by commas.

Ease of handling is excellent, passenger comfort is certainly above average, and fuel consumption is the lowest of all cars tested.

Introductory Expressions Such as *namely, for instance,* and *that is*

When introductory expressions (such as *namely, for instance, that is,* and *for example*) are used immediately following independent clauses, they may be preceded by either commas or semicolons. Generally, if the words following the introductory expression appear at the end of the sentence and form a series or an independent clause, use a semicolon before the introductory expression. If not, use a comma.

Numerous fringe benefits are available to employees; *namely,* stock options, life insurance, health insurance, dental care, and vision care. (A semicolon is used because *namely* introduces a series at the end of the sentence.)

Several books give additional information you may find useful when opening your own business; *for example,* Steve Mariotti's *The Young Entrepreneur's Guide to Starting and Running a Business* is an excellent resource. (A semicolon is used because *for example* introduces an independent clause.)

We are proposing many new additions to the health care package, *for example,* holistic medicine and chiropractic benefits. (A comma is used because *for example* introduces neither a series nor an independent clause.)

These same introductory expressions may introduce parenthetical words within sentences. Usually, commas punctuate parenthetical words within sentences. If the parenthetical words thus introduced are punctuated by internal commas, however, use dashes or parentheses. (Dashes and parentheses will be treated in detail in Chapter 13.)

The biggest health problems facing workers, *namely,* drug abuse and alcoholism, cost U.S. industry over $10 billion a year. (Commas are used because the parenthetical words contain only two items joined by *and.*)

The pursuit of basic job issues—*for instance,* wages, job security, and working conditions—has been the main concern of U.S. workers. (Dashes are used because the parenthetical words are punctuated with commas.)

Independent Clauses With Coordinating Conjunctions

Normally, a comma precedes a coordinating conjunction (*and, or, nor, but*) when it joins two independent clauses. If, however, either of the independent clauses contains additional commas and if the reader might be confused, a semicolon may be used instead of the normally expected comma.

We have forwarded your suggestions to our product manager, and he will consider them in future product-design decisions. (A comma precedes the coordinating conjunction because no additional punctuation appears within either clause.)

The first three cities recommended by our relocation committee were Atlanta, Dallas, and Cincinnati; but Miami, San Diego, and Seattle were also mentioned. (A semicolon precedes the coordinating conjunction to show where the second independent clause begins and to prevent confusion.)

GUIDELINES FOR USING COLONS

The colon is most often used to introduce formally listed items, quotations, and explanatory sentences.

Formally Listed Items

Use a colon after an independent clause that introduces one item, two items, or a formal list. A list may be shown vertically or horizontally and is usually introduced by such words as *the following, as follows, these,* or *thus.* A colon is also used when words like these are implied but not stated.

Creating a company Web site offered *the following* significant advantage: improved customer service. (Independent clause introduces single item.)

Some of the most commonly used manufacturers' discounts are *the following:* trade, cash, quantity, and seasonal. (Formal list with introductory expression stated)

Our company uses several delivery services for our important packages: UPS, FedEx, and USPS. (Formal list with introductory expression only implied)

These are a few of the services that a correspondent bank performs for other banks:

1. Collecting checks, payments, and other credit instruments
2. Accepting letters of credit and travelers' checks
3. Making credit investigations (Formal list shown vertically)

Do not use a colon unless the list is introduced by an independent clause. Lists often function as sentence complements or objects. When this is the case and the statement introducing the list is incomplete, no colon should be used. It might be easiest to remember that lists introduced by verbs or prepositions require no colons (because the introductory statement is incomplete).

Three requirements for this position *are* a master's degree, computer knowledge, and five years' experience in accounting. (No colon is used because the introductory statement is not complete; the list is introduced by a *to be* verb and functions as a complement to the sentence.)

Awards of merit were presented *to* Professor Loncorich, Ms. Harned, and Dr. Konishi. (No colon is used because the introductory statement is not an independent clause; the list functions as an object of the preposition *to*.)

Do not use a colon when an intervening sentence falls between the introductory statement and the list.

The following cities have been chosen as potential convention sites. A final decision will be made May 1.

New Orleans   San Francisco
Chicago   Orlando

(No colon appears after *sites* because an intervening sentence comes between the introductory statement and the list.)

Quotations

Use a colon to introduce long one-sentence quotations and quotations of two or more sentences.

Franklin D. Roosevelt said: "It is common sense to take a method and try it. If it fails, admit it freely and try another. But above all, try something."

Incomplete quotations not interrupting the flow of a sentence require no colon, no comma, and no initial capital letter.

The River Walk area of San Antonio is sometimes described as "the Venice of the Southwest."

Explanatory Sentences

Use a colon to separate two independent clauses if the second clause explains, illustrates, or supplements the first.

The company's new directors faced a perplexing dilemma: they had to choose between declaring bankruptcy and investing more funds to recoup previous losses. (The second clause explains what the *perplexing dilemma* is.)

One of the traits of highly successful people is this: they never give up on themselves. (The second clause explains what the *trait* is.)

Other Uses of the Colon

■ *After the salutation of a business letter*

> Dear Mr. Tarson: Dear Human Resources Manager: Dear Felicia:

■ *In expressions of time to separate hours from minutes*

> 10:15 a.m.   9:45 p.m.

■ *Between titles and subtitles*

> *High Tech Start Up: The Complete Handbook for Creating Successful New High Tech Companies*

■ *Between place of publication and name of publisher*

> Guffey, Mary Ellen, and Carolyn M. Seefer. *Essentials of College English.* 3d ed. Cincinnati: South-Western College Publishing, 2004.

Capitalization Following Colons

Do not capitalize the initial letter of words or of phrases listed following a colon unless the words so listed are proper nouns or appear as a vertical list.

> The qualities we are looking for in a manager are the following: experience, demonstrated management ability, product knowledge, and excellent communication skills.
>
> These cities will receive heavy promotional advertising: Omaha, Lincoln, Sioux City, and Council Bluffs.
>
> To be legally enforceable, a contract must include at least four elements:
> 1. Mutual assent of all parties
> 2. Parties who are competent
> 3. A consideration
> 4. A lawful purpose

Do not capitalize the first letter of an independent clause following a colon if that clause explains or supplements the first one (unless, of course, the first word is a proper noun).

> You will be interested in our new savings plan for one special reason: it allows you to invest up to $4,000 in a tax-free account.

Capitalize the first letter of an independent clause following a colon if that clause states a formal rule or principle.

> In business the Golden Rule is often stated in the following way: He with the gold rules.

For a quotation following a colon, capitalize the initial letter of each complete sentence.

> In their book *Clicks and Mortar,* David S. Pottruck and Terry Pierce say: "To distinguish one business from others, the people in the company have to be personally dedicated to the culture of the company. Their dedication needs to be such that they will automatically take the actions that make the company's culture live."

A FINAL WORD

Semicolons are excellent punctuation marks when used carefully and knowingly. After reading this chapter, though, some business communicators are guilty of semicolon overkill. They begin to string together two—and sometimes even three—independent clauses with semicolons. Remember to use semicolons in compound sentences ONLY when two ideas are better presented together.

You are now ready to complete the reinforcement exercises.

HOTLINE QUERIES

Q: **My partner and I are preparing an announcement describing our new Web business. We don't agree on how to punctuate this sentence:** *We offer a wide array of network services; such as design, support, troubleshooting, and consulting, etc.*

A: First, drop the semicolon before *such as*. No comma or semicolon is necessary before a list introduced by *such as*. Second, do not use *etc.* at the end of a series. If you have other services to offer, name them. Tacking on *etc.* suggests that you have more items but for some reason you are not listing them.

Q: **Which word should I use in this sentence?** *Our department will (disburse or disperse) the funds shortly.*

A: Use *disburse*. *Disperse* means "to scatter" (*Police dispersed the* *unruly crowd)* or "to distribute" *(Information will be dispersed to all divisions). Disburse* means "to pay out." Perhaps this memory device will help you keep them straight: associate the *b* in *disburse* with *bank (Banks disburse money).*

Q: **When I list items vertically, should I use a comma or a semicolon after each item? Should a period be used after the final item? For example,** *Please inspect the following rooms and equipment:*
1. *The control room*
2. *The power transformer and its standby*
3. *The auxiliary switchover equipment*

A: Do not use commas or semicolons after items listed vertically, and do not use a period after the last item in such a list. However, if the listed items are complete sentences or if they are long phrases that complete the meaning of the introductory comment, periods may be used after each item.

Q: **I'm writing a reply to a person who signed a letter** *J. R. Henderson.* **Since I don't know the person's gender, what should I use for the salutation?**

A: Use *Dear J. R. Henderson.*

Q: **I'm setting up advertising copy, and this sentence doesn't look right to me:** *This line of fishing reels are now priced . . . .*

A: Your suspicion is correct. The subject of the verb in this sentence is *line;* it requires the singular verb *is.*

Q: **I'm addressing a letter to the American Nurses Association. What salutation shall I use? One person in our office suggested** *Gentlewomen.* **Is this being used?**

A: We recommend that you use *Ladies and Gentlemen* since both male and female nurses are members of the association. In fact, this salutation is appropriate for any organization in which men and women may be represented in management. I would not use *Gentlewomen* because it sounds artificial. Businesses and individuals can avoid gender bias in language without using stilted constructions. Salutations such as *Dear Sir* and *Gentlemen* are no longer used. Today we are more sensitive to women as employees, managers, and executives. The use of awkward terms like *Gentlewomen* or *Gentlepersons,* however, is an overreaction and should be avoided. Probably the best approach is to write specific people. Find the name of the individual you should be addressing.

Q: **Why can't I remember how to spell** *already?* **I want to use it in this sentence:** *Your account has <u>already</u> been credited with your payment.*

HOTLINE QUERIES

A: You—and many others—have difficulty with *already* because two different words (and meanings) are expressed by essentially the same sounds. The adverb *already* means "previously" or "before this time," as in your sentence. The two-word combination *all ready* means "all prepared," as in *The club members are all ready to board the bus.* If you can logically insert the word *completely* between *all* and *ready,* you know the two-word combination is needed.

Q: I work in an office where we frequently send letters addressed to people on a first-name basis. Should I use a comma or a colon after a salutation like *Dear Antonio?*

A: The content of the letter, not the salutation (greeting), determines the punctuation after the salutation. If the letter is a business letter, always use a colon. If the letter is totally personal, a comma may be used, although a colon would also be appropriate.

Q: Another employee and I are collaborating on a report. I wanted to write this: *Money was lost due to poor attendance.* She says the sentence should read: *Money was lost because of poor attendance.* My version is more concise. Which of us is right?

A: Most language authorities agree with your coauthor. *Due to* is

acceptable when it functions as an adjective, as in *Success was due to proper timing.* In this sense, *due to* is synonymous with *attributable to.* However, when *due to* functions as a preposition, as in your sentence, language experts find fault. Your friend is right; substitute *because of.*

Q: I can never keep the words *capital* and *capitol* straight. Which one would I use in the sentence *He invested $150,000 of his own (capital, capitol) in his new business?*

A: This sentence requires the noun *capital,* which means "the wealth of an individual or firm." As a noun, *capital* is also used to refer to a city serving as the seat of government (*Albany is the capital of New York.*). As an adjective, *capital* is used to describe an uppercase letter (*capital letter*), something that is punishable by death (*capital punishment*), or something that is excellent (*a capital idea*). The noun *capitol* is used to describe a building used by the U.S. Congress (always capitalized) or a building where a state legislature meets (capitalized only when used in the full name of the building). Here are two examples: *They visited the United States Capitol Building on their recent trip to Washington, D.C. and admired its architecture. They had visited their state capitol building many times before their trip.*

13

OTHER PUNCTUATION

OBJECTIVES

When you have completed the material in this chapter, you will be able to do the following:

- Use periods to correctly punctuate statements, commands, indirect questions, polite requests, abbreviations, initials, and numerals.
- Use question marks and exclamation points correctly.
- Recognize acceptable applications of the dash.
- Use parentheses correctly.
- Explain when to use commas, dashes, or parentheses to set off nonessential material and correctly punctuate and capitalize material set off by parentheses and dashes.
- Correctly use double and single quotation marks and correctly place other punctuation marks in relation to quotation marks.
- Use underscores, italics, brackets, and apostrophes appropriately.

This chapter teaches you how to use periods, question marks, and exclamation points correctly. It also includes suggestions for punctuating with dashes, parentheses, single quotation marks, double quotation marks, underscores (italics), brackets, and apostrophes.

THE PERIOD

The period can be used to punctuate sentences, abbreviations, initials, and numerals. Guidelines for each use are covered in this section.

Never use more than one punctuation mark at the end of a sentence. If a sentence ends with an abbreviation, only one period is necessary.

To Punctuate Statements, Commands, and Indirect Questions

Use a period at the end of a statement, a command, or an indirect question.

> Ali Mazahri was promoted and his salary increased. (Statement)
> Deliver the food for the party before 5 p.m. (Command)
> Lindsay asked whether we had sent the price list. (Indirect question)

To Punctuate Polite Requests

Use a period at the end of a command, suggestion, or request phrased as a polite request. These requests ask the reader to perform a specific action instead of responding with a yes or no.

> Would you please send me your latest brochure. (Polite request)
> May I suggest that you follow the instructions in your manual. (Polite request)

Will you be sure to lock the door when you leave. (Polite request)

Could you check the latest prices on MP3 players. (Polite request)

If you are asking a favor or if you think the reader may feel that your request is presumptuous, use a question mark rather than a period.

May I ask you to fill in for me at the next board meeting? (Request that asks a favor)

If you are uncomfortable using a period at the end of a polite request, rephrase the sentence so that it is a statement:

Will you please mail your check in the enclosed envelope. (Polite request)

Please send your check in the enclosed envelope. (Polite request rephrased as a statement)

To Punctuate Abbreviations and Initials

Because of their inconsistencies, abbreviations present problems to writers. The following suggestions will help you organize certain groups of abbreviations and provide many models. In studying these models, note the spacing, capitalization, and use of periods. For a more thorough list of acceptable abbreviations, consult an up-to-date office reference manual or dictionary.

■ *Abbreviations using lowercase letters.* Use periods after many abbreviations beginning with lowercase letters.

a.m. (ante meridiem)	ft. (foot or feet)
e.g. (for example)	i.e. (that is)
et al. (and others)	p.m. (post meridiem)

Some exceptions: mph (miles per hour), wpm (words per minute), mm (millimeter), kg (kilogram), and km (kilometer).

■ *Abbreviations containing capital and lowercase letters.* Use periods for most abbreviations containing capital and lowercase letters.

Dr. (Doctor)	Mr. (Mister)
Esq. (Esquire)	Ms. (blend of Miss and Mrs.)
No. (number)	Sat. (Saturday)

■ *Abbreviations of academic degrees, geographical expressions, and initials.* Use periods with abbreviations that represent academic degrees, geographical expressions, and initials of a person's first and middle names.

A.A. (associate in arts)	R.O.C. (Republic of China)
B.S. (bachelor of science)	S.A. (South America)
M.B.A. (master of business administration)	U.K. (United Kingdom)
M.D. (doctor of medicine)	U.S.A. (United States of America)
Ph.D. (doctor of philosophy)	Mr. J. A. Jones (initials of name)

■ *Abbreviations containing all capital letters.* Do NOT use periods for most capitalized abbreviations. Capitalized abbreviations are often used for business organizations, educational institutions, governmental agencies, professional organizations, and business and technology terms.

Business organizations

AT&T (American Telephone and Telegraph)	IBM (International Business Machines)

Educational Institutions

UGA (University of Georgia)   UNC (University of North Carolina)

Governmental Agencies

EPA (Environmental Protection Agency)   SEC (Securities and Exchange Commission)

IRS (Internal Revenue Service)   USPS (U.S. Postal Service)

Professional Organizations

BBB (Better Business Bureau)   NOW (National Organization for Women)

IAAP (International Association of Administrative Professionals)   STC (Society for Technical Communication)

Business and Technology Terms

CEO (chief executive officer)   ID (identification)

CFO (chief financial officer)   ISP (Internet service provider)

CPA (certified public accountant)   PDF (portable document format)

CPU (central processing unit)   RAM (random-access memory)

DSL (digital subscriber line)   RSVP (respond if you please)

EST (Eastern Standard Time)   SASE (self-addressed, stamped envelope)

FYI (for your information)   SOP (standard operating procedure)

GAAP (generally accepted accounting principles)   UPC (Universal Product Code)

GDP (gross domestic product)   URL (Universal Resource Locator)

HTML (hypertext markup language)   WWW (World Wide Web)

HTTP (hypertext transfer protocol)   ZIP (or zip) (Zone Improvement Plan)

■ *Abbreviations for states and Canadian provinces.*   Do NOT use periods in two-letter state and Canadian province abbreviations. These abbreviations should also use capitalized letters and tight spacing. For a complete list of two-letter state and Canadian province abbreviations, consult an office reference manual.

AR (Arkansas)   FL (Florida)

AK (Alaska)   HI (Hawaii)

CA (California)   NS (Nova Scotia)

■ *Abbreviations with two forms.*   Some abbreviations have two acceptable forms.

a.k.a., AKA (also known as)   e.o.m., EOM (end of month)

c.o.d., COD (collect on delivery)   f.o.b., FOB (free on board)

d.b.a., DBA (doing business as)   p.o.e., POE (port of entry)

To Punctuate Numerals

For a monetary sum use a period (decimal point) to separate dollars from cents.

> The two items in question, $13.92 and $98.67, were both charged in the month of October.

Use a period (decimal point) to mark a decimal fraction.

> Only 35.3 percent of eligible voters voted in Tuesday's election.

Spacing After Periods

When typewriters and printers used monospaced fonts, typists were taught to leave two spaces after a period at the end of a sentence. Two spaces provided a strong visual break so that the end of the sentence was apparent. With modern proportional fonts, however, this added visual break is unnecessary. Most typists leave only one space after terminal periods today. A two-space break is equally acceptable, especially when misreading may occur. For example, when abbreviations appear at the end of one sentence and the beginning of the next, two spaces prevent confusion (*Your appointment is at 2 p.m. Dr. Wiley will see you then.*) The same spacing guidelines apply to other end punctuation (question marks and exclamation points), which will be discussed in the next two sections.

THE QUESTION MARK

In addition to ending a direct question, the question mark can be used to punctuate questions appended to statements and to indicate doubt. The guidelines for these uses are covered in this section.

To Punctuate Direct Questions

Use a question mark at the end of a direct question.

> What can we do to improve communication among departments?
> Has the music industry been successful in stopping illegal file sharers?

To Punctuate Questions Appended to Statements

Place a question mark after a question that is appended to a statement. Use a comma to separate the statement from the question.

> McDonald's has already installed wireless Internet networks (Wi-Fis) in many locations, hasn't it?
> This order should be sent by e-mail, don't you think?

To Indicate Doubt

A question mark within parentheses may be used to indicate a degree of doubt about some aspect of a statement.

> Each application should be accompanied by two (?) letters of recommendation.
> After the dot-com was launched (2001?), it immediately experienced financial difficulties.

THE EXCLAMATION POINT

Because the exclamation point is used to express strong emotion, it should be used sparingly in professional writing.

To Express Strong Emotion

After a word, phrase, or clause expressing strong emotion, use an exclamation point.

> Impossible! I will never be able to meet such a tight deadline.
> Unbelievable! Have you seen these sales figures?
> What a day! Will 5 p.m. never come?

Do not use an exclamation point after mild interjections, such as *oh* and *well*.

> Well, I was expecting something like this.
> Oh, now I see what you mean.

THE DASH

The dash is a legitimate and effective mark of punctuation when used according to accepted conventions. As an emphatic punctuation mark, however, the dash loses effectiveness when it is overused. In typewritten or simple word processing–generated material, a dash is formed by typing two hyphens with no space before, between, or after the hyphens. In printed or desktop publishing-generated material, a dash appears as a solid line (an *em* dash). Most current word processors will automatically convert two hyphens to an *em* dash. Study the following suggestions for and illustrations of appropriate uses of the dash.

To Set Off Parenthetical Elements

Within a sentence parenthetical elements are usually set off by commas. If, however, the parenthetical element itself contains internal commas, use dashes (or parentheses) to set it off.

> Sources of raw materials—farming, mining, fishing, and forestry—are all dependent on energy.
> Four legal assistants—Priscilla Alvarez, Anna Billy, Yoshiki Ono, and Eli Greenstein—received cash bonuses for outstanding performance in their departments.

To Indicate an Interruption

An interruption or abrupt change of thought may be separated from the rest of a sentence by a dash.

> We will refund your money—you have my guarantee—if you are not satisfied.
> You can submit your report on Friday—no, we must have it by Thursday at the latest.

Sentences with abrupt changes of thought or with appended afterthoughts can usually be improved through rewriting.

To Set Off a Summarizing Statement

Use a dash (not a colon) to separate an introductory list from a summarizing statement.

> Flexibility, communication skills, patience—these are the qualities I appreciate most in a manager.
> Cal Bears, Georgia Bulldogs, Michigan State Spartans—those are Chip's favorite college football teams.

To Attribute a Quotation

Place a dash between a quotation and its source.

> "Live as if you were to die tomorrow. Learn as if you were to live forever."
> —Mahatma Gandhi
> "The future belongs to those who believe in the beauty of their dreams."
> —Eleanor Roosevelt

PARENTHESES

Parentheses are generally used in pairs. This section covers guidelines for using parentheses correctly.

To Set Off Nonessential Sentence Elements

Generally, nonessential sentence elements may be punctuated as follows: (a) with commas, to make the lightest possible break in the normal flow of a sentence; (b) with dashes, to emphasize the enclosed material; and (c) with parentheses, to de-emphasize the enclosed material.

> Figure 17, which appears on page 9, clearly illustrates the process involved. (Normal punctuation.)
> Figure 17—which appears on page 9—clearly illustrates the process involved. (Dashes emphasize enclosed material.)
> Figure 17 (which appears on page 9) clearly illustrates the process involved. (Parentheses de-emphasize enclosed material.)

Explanations, references, and directions are often enclosed in parentheses.

> The bank's current business hours (9 a.m. to 5 p.m.) will be extended in the near future (to 6 p.m.).
> I recommend that we direct more funds (see the budget on p. 14) to research and development.
> The Shanghai real estate tycoon bought the twin turbo shiny blue Bentley for 4.68 million yuan ($566,093) in cash.

To Mark Numerals and Enumerated Items

Legal, business, and professional documents often show numerals in both written and figure form for clarity. When this is done, the figure form is often placed in parentheses.

> Your final installment payment is due in ninety (90) days.
> The board has decided to accept your bid of one hundred nine thousand five hundred dollars ($109,500) for the construction project.

When using numbers or letters to enumerate lists within sentences, enclose the numbers or letters in parentheses. Use letters for items that have no particular order. Use numbers for items that suggest a sequence.

> The Federal Trade Commission (FTC) has initiated several programs to protect individual privacy, including (a) the National Do Not Call Registry, (b) the Fair Credit Reporting Act, and (c) an identity theft Web site.
> To post your résumé online, (1) prepare and save your résumé using your word processor, (2) log in to your Monster.com account, (3) click the *Résumé* link, (4) click the *Attach an Existing Résumé* link, (5) type in a résumé headline and career objective, (6) attach your résumé, and (7) click the *Save* button.

Additional Considerations

If the material enclosed by parentheses is embedded within another sentence, a question mark or exclamation point may be used where normally expected. Do not, however, use a period after a statement embedded within another sentence.

I visited the new business travel Web site (have you seen it?) last night. (A question mark concludes a question enclosed by parentheses and embedded in another sentence.)

We held a special meeting (but no one attended it!) to discuss these policy issues. (An exclamation mark concludes an exclamation enclosed by parentheses and embedded in another sentence.)

Photoshop Element's "hints palette" feature (see Chapter 5) provides helpful illustrations and tips. (A period is not used at the end of a statement that is enclosed by parentheses and embedded in another sentence.)

If the material enclosed by parentheses is not embedded in another sentence, use whatever punctuation is required.

Our proposal is to hire eight new employees immediately to keep the project on track. (See Appendix A for job descriptions and associated costs.)

An estimated two thirds of U.S. employees work in the services sector. (Does anyone remember when most jobs were in manufacturing?)

In sentences involving expressions within parentheses, a comma, semicolon, or colon that would normally occupy the position occupied by the second parenthesis is then placed after that parenthesis.

When we deliver the product (in late June), we can begin testing on site. (Comma follows parenthesis.)

Your tax return was received before the deadline (April 15); however, you did not include a payment. (Semicolon follows parenthesis.)

QUOTATION MARKS

Guidelines for using quotation marks to enclose direct quotations, quotations within quotations, short expressions, definitions, and literary titles are covered in this section. You will also learn how to place other punctuation in relation to quotation marks.

To Enclose Direct Quotations

Double quotation marks are used to enclose direct quotations. Unless the exact words of a writer or speaker are being repeated, however, quotation marks are not employed.

"Never trust a computer you can't throw out a window," said Apple Computer Corporation cofounder Steve Wozniak. (Direct quotation enclosed)

Abraham Lincoln said that we cannot escape tomorrow's responsibility by evading it today. (An indirect quotation requires no quotation marks.)

Capitalize only the first word of a direct quotation.

"The human race has one really effective weapon," said Mark Twain, "and that is laughter." (Do not capitalize *and*.)

To Enclose Quotations Within Quotations

Single quotation marks (apostrophes on most keyboards) are used to enclose quoted passages cited within quoted passages.

My boss said, "I agree with Woody Allen, who said, 'Eighty percent of success is showing up.'" (Single quotation marks within double quotation marks)

To Enclose Short Expressions

Slang, words used in a special sense, and words following *stamped* or *marked* are often enclosed within quotation marks.

> Cheryl feared that her presentation would "bomb." (Slang)
> Computer criminals are often called "hackers." (Words used in a special sense)
> Some companies are employing Web logs, better known as "blogs," to improve the flow of information among employees. (Words used in a special sense)
> The package was stamped "Handle with Care." (Words following *stamped*)

To Enclose Definitions

Quotation marks are used to enclose definitions of words or expressions. The word or expression being defined should be underscored or set in italics.

> The French term *fait accompli* means "an accomplished deed or fact."
> Business owners use the term *working capital* to indicate an "excess of current assets over current debts."

To Enclose Titles

Quotation marks are used to enclose the titles of subdivisions of literary and artistic works, such as magazine and newspaper articles, chapters of books, episodes of television shows, poems, lectures, and songs. However, italics (or underscores) are used to enclose the titles of complete works, such as the names of books, magazines, pamphlets, movies, television series, albums, and newspapers.

> I loved the article in *The Wall Street Journal* entitled "Why Does 'Everybody' Now Put 'Everything' in Quotation Marks?"
> One source of information for your proposal might be the magazine article "The ADA's Next Step: Cyberspace," which appeared in *BusinessWeek* recently.
> Job seekers find the section entitled "The Impatient Job-Hunter" from *What Color Is Your Parachute?* very helpful.
> The *Friends* episode "The One With the Blind Date," in which Joey and Phoebe play matchmaker with Rachel and Ross, featured guest star Jon Lovitz.
> *Vertigo* was filmed almost entirely on location in San Francisco.

Additional Punctuation Considerations

Periods and commas are always placed inside closing quotation marks, whether single or double. Semicolons and colons, on the other hand, are always placed outside quotation marks.

> Angie said, "I'm sure the package was stamped 'First Class.'"
> The article is entitled "Corporate Espionage," but I don't have a copy.
> Our contract stipulated that "both parties must accept arbitration as binding"; therefore, the decision reached by the arbitrators is final.
> Three dates have been scheduled for the seminar called "Successful E-Business": April 1, May 3, and June 5.

Question marks and exclamation points may go inside or outside closing quotation marks, as determined by the form of the quotation.

> Meenu Kapai said, "How may I apply for that position?" (The quotation is a question.)
> "If your cell phone rings again," fumed the committee chair, "we will ask you to leave!" (The quotation is an exclamation.)

Do you know who it was who said, "When you cease to dream, you cease to live"? (The incorporating sentence asks the question; the quotation does not.)

I can't believe that the check was stamped "Insufficient Funds"! (The incorporating sentence is an exclamation; the quotation is not.)

When did the manager say, "Who wants to schedule a summer vacation?" (Both the incorporating sentence and the quotation are questions. Use only one question mark inside the quotation marks.)

UNDERSCORE AND ITALICS

The underscore or italics are normally used for titles of books, magazines, newspapers, television shows, movies, and other complete works published separately. In addition, words under discussion in the sentence and used as nouns are italicized or underscored.

If You Think You're Not Buying It, You Probably Are, the latest book by author Joe Cappo, was favorably reviewed in *The Wall Street Journal.*

They saw *Terminator 3: Rise of the Machines* on opening night

My favorite Frank Sinatra song is "You Make Me Feel So Young" from the *Songs for Swingin' Lovers!* album.

Two of the most frequently misused words are *affect* and *effect.* (Words used as nouns.)

BRACKETS

Within quotations, brackets are used by writers to enclose their own inserted remarks. Such remarks may be corrective, illustrative, or explanatory. Brackets are also used within quotations to enclose the word *sic,* which means "thus" or "so." This Latin form is used to emphasize the fact that an error obvious to all actually appears *thus* in the quoted material.

"A British imperial gallon," reported Ms. Sohoori, "is equal to 1.2 U.S. gallons [4.54 liters]."

"The company's reorganization program," wrote President Todd Holt, "will have its greatest affect [sic] on our immediate sales."

STUDY TIP

With today's sophisticated software programs and printers, you can, like professional printers, use italics instead of underscoring for titles and special words.

THE APOSTROPHE

As you have already learned, the apostrophe is used to form possessives and contractions. The apostrophe can also be used to take the place of omitted letters and as a symbol for *feet.* The guidelines for these uses are covered in this section.

To Form Noun Possessives

In Chapter 2 you learned that the apostrophe can be used to make common and proper nouns possessive. Do not use the apostrophe to make nouns plural.

She didn't understand her *boss's* instructions.

Today's software requires more processing power.

The Harrises' small consulting firm is thriving.

The *companies'* attorneys are evaluating the merger agreement. (Notice that *companies'* is a plural word showing possession, whereas *attorneys* is merely plural.)

To Form Contractions

Chapter 3 illustrated how to use the apostrophe to form contractions, which are shortened forms of subjects and verbs. Don't confuse contractions with pronouns.

> *It's* too early to determine if *we'll* make a profit this year. (*It's* represents *it is*; *we'll* represents *we will*.)
> *You're* invited to show us your portfolio next week. (*You're* represents *you are*.)
> *I've* no way of knowing if *there's* a solution to this problem (*I've* represents *I have*; *there's* represents *there is*.)
> *You'd* be happier if you *didn't* complain so much. (*You'd* represents *You would*; *didn't* represents *did not*.)

To Take the Place of Omitted Letters or Figures

The apostrophe can be used to take the place of omitted letters or figures. This is especially common when expressing a year.

> Music, films, and fashions of the *'70s* are suddenly popular again.
> Job prospects for the class of *'06* look very promising.
> He stops by *Dunkin'* Donuts on his way to work every morning.

To Serve as the Symbol for *feet*

In technical documents the apostrophe can be used as the symbol for *feet*. (A quotation mark is used as the symbol for *inches*.)

> The conference room is 14' × 16'. (14 feet by 16 feet)
> She is only 5' 1", but she can overpower a room. (5 feet, 1 inch)

You are now ready to complete the reinforcement exercises.

HOTLINE QUERIES

Q: My team and I are writing a proposal in which we say that *some of the current dot coms are undervalued*. We can't agree on how to write *dot coms*.

A: This playful reference to Internet companies is a little slangy, but we are hearing it more and more often. You could write it *dot.com*, but that's like saying *dot dot com*. We suggest using *dot-com* to avoid the obvious redundancy.

Q: I have a question about the use of *etc.* in this sentence: *We are installing better lighting, acoustical tile, sound barriers, and etc.* Should I use two periods at the end of the sentence, and does a comma precede *etc.?*

A: Although the use of *etc.* (meaning "and so forth") is generally avoided, do not, if it is to be used, include the redundant word *and*. When *etc.* is found at the end of a sentence, one comma should precede it. When *etc.* appears in the middle of a sentence, two commas should set it off. For example, *Better lighting, acoustical tile, and sound barriers, etc., are being installed.* NEVER use two periods at the end of a sentence, even if the sentence ends with an abbreviation such as *etc.*

Q: **We can't decide whether the period should go inside quotation marks or outside. At the end of a sentence, I have typed the title "Positive Vs. Negative Values." The author of the document that I'm typing wants the period outside because she says the title does not have a period in it.**

A: In the United States typists and printers have adopted a uniform style: when a period or comma falls at the same place quotation marks would normally fall, the period or comma is always placed inside the quotation marks—regardless of the content of the quotation. In Britain a different style is observed.

Q: **I'm not sure where to place the question mark in this sentence:** *His topic will be* **"What Is a Good Health Plan (?)"** **Does the question mark go inside the quotation marks? Too, should a comma precede the title of the talk?**

A: First, a question mark goes inside the quotation mark because the quoted material is in the form of a question. Be sure that you do not use another end punctuation mark after the quotation mark. Second, do not use a comma preceding the title of the topic because the sentence follows normal subject-verb-complement order. No comma is needed to separate the verb and the complement.

Q: **Should a hyphen be used in the word** *dissimilar?*

A: No. Prefixes such as *dis, pre, non, re,* and *un* do not require hyphens. Even when the final letter of the prefix is repeated in the initial letter of the root word, no hyphens are used: *disspirited, preenroll, nonnutritive, reestablish.*

Q: **At the end of a letter I wrote:** *Thank you for attending to this matter immediately.* **Should I hyphenate** *thank you?*

A: Do not hyphenate *thank you* when using it as a verb (*thank you for writing*). Do use hyphens when using it as an adjective (*I sent a thank-you note*) or as a noun (*I sent four thank-yous*). Since *thank you* is used as a verb in your sentence, do not hyphenate it. Notice that *thank you* is never written as a single word.

HOTLINE QUERIES

Q: **Where should the word *sic* be placed when it is used?**

A: *Sic* means "thus" or "so stated," and it is properly placed immediately following the word or phrase to which it refers. For example, *The kidnappers placed a newspaper advertisement that read "Call Monna [sic] Lisa." Sic* is used within a quotation to indicate that a quoted word or phrase, though inaccurately spelled or used, appeared thus in the original. *Sic* is italicized and placed within brackets.

Q: **Should *undercapitalized* be hyphenated? I can't find it in my dictionary.**

A: The prefixes *under* and *over* are not followed by hyphens.

Q: **I just checked the dictionary and found that *cooperate* is now written as one word. It seems to me that years ago it was *co-operate* or *coöperate*. Has the spelling changed?**

A: Yes, it has. The hyphen is no longer used in most words beginning with the prefix *co* (*coauthor, cocounsel, codesign, cofeature, cohead, copilot, costar, cowrite*). Only a few words retain the hyphen (*co-anchor, co-edition, co-official*). Check your dictionary for usage. In reading your dictionary, notice that centered periods are used to indicate syllables (*co·work·er*); hyphens are used to show hyphenated syllables (*co-own*).

The spelling of many other words has changed also. As new words become more familiar, their spelling tends to become more simplified. For example, *per cent* and *good will* are now shown by most dictionaries as *percent* and *goodwill*. By the same token, many words formerly hyphenated are now written without hyphens: *strike-over* is now *strikeover*, *to-day* is *today*, *to-morrow* is *tomorrow*, *editor-in-chief* is *editor in chief*, *vice-president* is *vice president*, and *passer-by* is now *passerby*. Current dictionaries reflect these changes.

Q: **I sometimes see three periods in a row in documents I'm reading and in book and film reviews. Does this use of periods have a name? When is this type of punctuation used?**

A: A series of three periods, with spaces before, between, and after each period, is called an *ellipsis* (...). Ellipses are usually used to show that information has been left out of quoted material. (*Roger Ebert's review of* Chicago *includes these words:* "By filming it in its own spirit, by making it frankly a stagy song-and-dance revue . . . the movie is big, brassy fun.") The ellipsis shows that this is not Roger Ebert's complete quote and that words have been omitted between *revue* and *the*.

14

CAPITALIZATION

OBJECTIVES

When you have completed the material in this chapter, you will be able to do the following:

- Determine when to capitalize beginning words of sentences, quoted sentences, components of business correspondence, independent phrases, vertically listed items, words following *marked* and *stamped,* and rules or principles following colons
- Distinguish between common and proper nouns for purposes of capitalization.
- Decide when to capitalize proper adjectives and when not to.
- Properly capitalize abbreviations, geographic locations, and points of the compass.
- Correctly capitalize the names of organizations, products, departments, divisions, and committees.
- Understand when to capitalize government terms, personal and professional titles, academic courses and degrees, and seasons.
- Apply capitalization rules to published and artistic titles, celestial bodies, ethnic and religious references, and numbered and lettered items.

Rules governing capitalization reflect conventional practices; that is, they have been established by custom and usage. By following these conventions, a writer tells a reader, among other things, what words are important. In earlier times writers capitalized most nouns and many adjectives at will; few conventions of capitalization or punctuation were then consistently observed. Today most capitalization follows definite rules that are fully accepted and practiced at all times. Dictionaries are helpful in determining capitalization practices, but they do not show all capitalized words. To develop skill in controlling capitals, study the rules and examples shown in this chapter.

RULES OF CAPITALIZATION

Beginning Words

In addition to capitalizing the first word of a complete sentence, capitalize the first words in quoted sentences, some components of business correspondence, independent phrases, vertically listed items, words following *marked* and *stamped,* and formal rules or principles following colons

- ***Capitalize the first letter of a word beginning a sentence.***

    Inventory and sales data are transmitted electronically.

- ***Capitalize the first words in quoted sentences.***

    James Joyce said, "Mistakes are portals of discovery."

- *Capitalize the first letter in independent phrases.*

  No, not at the present time.

- *Capitalize the first word of certain business correspondence components (letters, memos, and e-mail messages.*

  SUBJECT: Monthly Sales Meeting on June 9 (Capitalize the first letter of all primary words in a *subject line;* an alternative is to type the subject line in all capital letters.)

  Dear Mr. Hemingway: (Capitalize the first word and all nouns in a *salutation.*)

  Sincerely yours, (Capitalize the first word of a *complimentary close;* do not capitalize any words that follow.)

- *Capitalize the first words in vertically listed items.*

  Big utilities formed an alliance to sell the following:
  1. Electricity
  2. Natural gas
  3. Energy management services

- *Capitalize words that follow the words* marked *and* stamped.

  Although it was stamped "Fragile," the box failed to protect the fragile computer components.

  The check came back marked "Insufficient Funds."

- *Capitalize formal rules or principles following colons.*

  Our office manager repeated his favorite rule: Follow the company stylebook for correct capitalization.

Proper Nouns

Capitalize proper nouns, including the *specific* names of persons, places, schools, streets, parks, buildings, religions, holidays, months, nicknames, agreements, and so forth. Do NOT capitalize common nouns that make *general* reference.

PROPER NOUNS	COMMON NOUNS
Sam Chapman	a young man on the staff
Mexico, Canada	neighboring countries of the United States
Foothill College, University of Miami	a community college and a university
Pac Bell Park, Fenway Park	baseball parks
Episcopalian, Methodist	representatives of two religions
Sycamore Room, Fairmont Hotel	a room in the hotel
Veterans Day, New Year's Day	two holidays
Golden Gate Bridge, Brooklyn Bridge	bridges over bodies of water
Empire State Building	a building in a city
Supreme Court, Congress	components of government
October, November, December	last three months of the year
Monday, Tuesday, Sunday	three days of the week
the Windy City, the Big Apple	nicknames of cities
North American Free Trade Agreement	an agreement between countries
Lombard Street, Fifth Avenue	two famous streets
PowerPoint, WordPerfect	software programs
eBay, The Grammar Lady Online	Web sites
Industrial Revolution, Digital Age	periods of time

Proper Adjectives

Capitalize most adjectives that are derived from proper nouns.

Renaissance art	Socratic method
Keynesian economics	Belgian waffle
Freudian slip	British rock
Heimlich maneuver	Spanish language
Indian rupee	Internet service provider

Do not capitalize those adjectives originally derived from proper nouns that have become common adjectives (without capitals) through usage. Consult your dictionary when in doubt.

venetian blinds	epicurean feast
plaster of paris	french fries
india ink	diesel engine
manila folder	china dishes
mandarin collar	homburg hat
monarch butterfly	charley horse

Abbreviations

As you learned in Chapter 13, many organizations, educational institutions, and governmental agencies use abbreviations that are written in all capital letters. In addition, the abbreviations of many business and technology terms are written in all uppercase letters. Finally, the two-letter state and Canadian province abbreviations should be written using all capital letters.

GE (General Electric)	UCLA (University of California, Los Angeles)
CIA (Central Intelligence Agency)	AMA (American Medical Association)
PBS (Public Broadcasting Service)	NPR (National Public Radio)
PIN (personal identification number)	RAM (random-access memory)
MT (Montana)	BC (British Columbia)

Geographic Locations

Capitalize the names of *specific* places such as states, cities, mountains, valleys, lakes, rivers, oceans, and geographic regions. Capitalize *county* and *state* when they follow the proper nouns.

Maine, New Hampshire, Vermont	Snake River, Mississippi River
Kansas City, Minneapolis	Atlantic Ocean, Arctic Ocean
Mount Lassen, Mount Everest	Lake Louise, Dead Sea
Death Valley, Yosemite Valley	Pacific Northwest, Texas Panhandle
New York State, Monroe County	European Community (EC)

Do not capitalize words such as *city of, state of,* and *county of* when they come before the geographic locations they are describing.

city of Chicago	state of Washington
county of Contra Costa	town of Cape Vincent

STUDY TIP

A clue to the capitalization of a region is the use of *the* preceding it: *the East Coast, the West, the Pacific Northwest.*

Points of the Compass

Capitalize *north, south, east, west,* and their derivatives (*northeast, southwest,* etc.) when they represent *specific* regions.

the Middle East, the Far East	the Midwest, the Pacific Northwest
the East Coast, the West Coast	Easterners, Southerners
Northern Hemisphere	Northern California, South Georgia

Do not capitalize the points of the compass when they are used in directions or in general references.

turn east on Guadalupe Parkway	north California, southern Georgia
to the west of town	in the northern Rockies
drive south on Highway 1	eastern Washington, western Maryland

Organization Names

SPOT THE BLOOPER

From an AP story about a lawsuit filed by a woman who said she was burned by a pickle that fell out of her McDonald's burger: "While attempting to eat the hamburger, the pickle dropped from the hamburger onto her chin."

Capitalize the principal words in the names of all business, civic, educational, governmental, labor, military, philanthropic, political, professional, religious, and social organizations.

United States Air Force	American Heart Association
Better Business Bureau	Pasadena Unified School District
Habitat for Humanity	Microsoft Corporation
Securities and Exchange Commission	Federal Reserve Board
Screen Actors Guild	Green Party
United Farm Workers of America	National Football Association
National Park Service	The Boeing Company*

DID YOU KNOW?

One of the most widely publicized legal battles over trademark protection involved Parker Brothers. It threatened to sue an economics professor at San Francisco State University for naming his new board game "Anti-Monopoly." After nine years of litigation, courts stripped "Monopoly" of trademark protection, thus making the name generic.

Generally, do NOT capitalize *company, association, board,* and other shortened name forms when they are used to replace full organization names. If these shortened names, however, are preceded by the word *the* and are used in formal or legal documents (contracts, bylaws, minutes, etc.), they may be capitalized.

The *company* is moving its headquarters to Carbondale, Illinois. (Informal document.)
The Treasurer of the *Association* is herein authorized to disburse funds. (Formal document.)

Product Names

DID YOU KNOW?

The words *corn flakes, escalator, PC* (as in *personal computer*), and *raisin bran* all were once trademarks but have slipped into common use. The Coca-Cola Company reportedly employs eight full-time attorneys who do nothing but watch over its trademark. Why such protection? Companies have huge marketing investments in their trademarks.

Capitalize product names only when they represent trademarked items. Except in advertising, common names following manufacturers' names are not capitalized.

Coca-Cola	DuPont Teflon	Nikon SLR camera
Kleenex tissues	Xerox copier	NordicTrack Walkfit
Magic Marker	Maytag washer	Styrofoam cup
Amana Radarange	IBM computer	Jeep Cherokee
Q-Tips	Frigidaire refrigerator	Formica counter
Iomega Zip disk	Excel spreadsheet	Kodak film

---

*Capitalize *the* only when it is part of an organization's official name (as it would appear on the organization's stationery).

Departments, Divisions, and Committees

Capitalize the names of departments, divisions, or committees within your own organization. Outside your organization capitalize only *specific* department, division, or committee names.

> Contact our Client Support Department for more information.
> He works with the International Division of Apple.
> You have been appointed to the Process Improvement Committee.
> Send your employment application to their human resources department.
> A steering committee has not yet been named.

Governmental Terms

Do not capitalize the words *federal, government, nation,* or *state* unless they are part of a specific title.

> Neither the state government nor the federal government would fund the proposal.
> The Federal Trade Commission regulates advertising in all the states.

Titles of People

Many rules exist for capitalizing personal and professional titles of people.

■ ***Titles preceding names.*** Capitalize courtesy titles (such as *Mr., Mrs., Ms., Miss,* and *Dr.)* when they precede names. Also capitalize titles representing a person's profession, company position, military rank, religious station, political office, family relationship, or nobility when the titles precedes the name and replaces a courtesy title.

> The staff greeted *Mr. and Mrs.* Gary Smith. (Courtesy titles)
> Speakers included *Professor* Suzanne Miller and *Dr.* Jackie Harless-Chang. (Professional titles)
> Sales figures were submitted by *Budget Director* Magaldi and *Vice President* Anderson. (Company titles)
> Will *Major General* Donald M. Franklin assume command? (Military title)
> Appearing together were *Rabbi* David Cohen, *Archbishop* Sean McKee, and *Reverend* Thomas White. (Religious titles)
> We expect *President* Bush to offer support for *Senator* Tom Watson and *Mayor* Warren Rivers in the next campaign. (Political titles)
> Only *Aunt* Brenda and *Uncle* Skip had been to Alaska. (Family relationship)
> Onlookers waited for *Prince* Charles and *Queen* Elizabeth to arrive. (Nobility)

■ ***Titles followed by appositives.*** Do not capitalize a person's title—professional, business, military, religious, political, family, or one related to nobility—when the title is followed by an appositive. You will recall that appositives rename or explain previously mentioned nouns or pronouns.

> Only one *professor,* Jane Connelly, favored a tuition hike.
> Republican candidates asked their *president,* George W. Bush, to help raise funds.
> Reva Hillman discovered that her *uncle,* Paul Royka, had named her as his heir.

■ ***Titles or offices following names.*** Do not capitalize titles or offices following names.

> Leon Jones, *president* of Allied Chemical, met with Cathy Verrett, *director* of Human Resources.
> After repeated requests, Rose Valenzuela, *supervisor,* Document Services, announced extended hours.

George W. Bush, *president* of the United States, confronted Robert Hollingsworth, *senator* from Wyoming.

William H. Renquist, *chief justice* of the Supreme Court, promised a ruling in June.

■ **Titles or offices replacing names.** Generally, do not capitalize a title or office that replaces a person's name.

Neither the *president* of the company nor the *executive vice president* could be reached for comment.

An ambitious five-year plan was developed by the *director of marketing* and the *sales manager.*

The *president* conferred with the *joint chiefs of staff* and the *secretary of defense.*

At the reception the *mayor* of Providence spoke with the *governor* of Vermont.

■ **Titles in an organization's minutes, bylaws, or other official documents.** When a title of an official appears in that organization's minutes, bylaws, or other official document, it may be capitalized.

The Controller will have authority over departmental budgets. (Title appearing in bylaws)

By vote of the stockholders, the President is empowered to implement a stock split. (Title appearing in annual report)

■ **Titles used with terms ex, elect, late, and former.** When the terms *ex, elect, late,* and *former* are used with capitalized titles, they are not capitalized.

We went to hear ex-President Carter speak at the symposium.

Mayor-elect Newsom proposed a city council meeting for next week.

We just learned that former President Clinton will speak on campus next month.

■ **Titles used alone.** Titles other than *sir, ladies,* and *gentlemen* are capitalized when used alone in direct address.

I hope, Doctor, that you will be able to see me today.

Welcome, ladies and gentlemen, to our grand opening.

We can seat you right away, sir.

■ **Titles in addresses and closing lines of business correspondence.** Capitalize titles in addresses and closing lines of business correspondence.

Ms. Maria Giuili   Sincerely yours,
Executive Vice President, Planning
Energy Systems Technology, Inc.
8907 Canoga Avenue   Lisa W. Greenway
Canoga Park, CA 91371   Marketing Manager

■ **Family titles.** Do not capitalize family titles used with possessive pronouns.

my mother   our aunt
his father   your cousin

But do capitalize titles of close relatives when they are used without pronouns.

Please call Father immediately.

What do you think about my decision, Mom?

Academic Courses and Degrees

Course titles with numbers are usually capitalized (*Marketing 101*). Those without numbers usually are not capitalized (*marketing*).

Capitalize the names of numbered courses and specific course titles. Do not capitalize the names of academic subject areas unless they contain a proper noun.

> Marie plans to take Keyboarding I, Math 128, and Accounting 181 next semester.
> Anna excelled in business management, Japanese, and computer programming.
> All accounting majors must take business English and business law.

Capitalize abbreviations of academic degrees whether they stand alone or follow individuals' names. Do not capitalize general references to degrees.

> Cathy Overby earned B.S., M.S., and Ph.D. degrees before her thirtieth birthday. (Bachelor of Science, Master of Science, and Doctor of Philosophy degrees)
> Matthew hopes to earn bachelor's and master's degrees in business administration. (General reference to degrees)
> Lynn Spiesel, M.S., manages my department.
> New employees include Tracey Barry, Ph.D., and John Finger, M.Ed.

Headline in *The Washington Times:* "Threat of espionage hinder Paris air show."

Seasons

Do not capitalize seasons unless they are personified (spoken of as if alive).

> Our annual sales meeting is held each spring.
> She plans to return to school in the fall.
> "Come, Winter, with thine angry howl . . ."—Burns

SPOT THE BLOOPER

From an animal rights group's advertisement showing a photo of a cat and a pig: "Who do you pet and who do you eat?"

Published and Artistic Titles

Capitalize the principal words in the titles of books, magazines, newspapers, articles, movies, plays, songs, poems, and reports. Do NOT capitalize articles (*a, an, the*), conjunctions with three or fewer letters (*and, but, or, nor*), and prepositions with three or fewer letters (*in, to, by, for,* etc.) unless they begin or end the title. The word *to* in infinitives (*to run, to say, to write*) is also not capitalized unless it appears as the first word of a title or subtitle.

By the way, remember from what you learned in Chapter 13 that the titles of published works that contain subdivisions (such as books, magazines, pamphlets, newspapers, TV series, movies, albums, plays, musicals, and Web sites) are italicized or underscored. Titles of literary or artistic works without subdivisions (such as book chapters, magazine articles, newspaper articles, songs, acts in a play, poems, links on Web sites, and episodes in a TV series) are placed in quotation marks.

> Robert K. Greenleaf's *On Becoming a Servant-Leader* (Book)
> Roger Fisher's *Getting to Yes: Negotiating Agreement Without Giving In* (Book)
> *The Wall Street Journal* (Newspaper)
> *Late Night With David Letterman* (TV series)
> *The Sound of Music* (Movie)
> *Phantom of the Opera* (Play)
> Bob Dylan's "When the Ship Comes In" on *The Times They Are A-Changin'* (Song and album)
> "Can Online Investing Work for You?" (Magazine article)
> Robert Frost's "Stopping by Woods on a Snowy Evening" (Poem)
> "Career Development," a link at *Hoover's Online* (Link and Web site)

Celestial Bodies

Capitalize the names of celestial bodies such as Jupiter, Saturn, and Neptune. Do not capitalize the terms *earth, sun,* or *moon* unless they appear in a context with other celestial bodies.

> Where on earth did you find that ancient typewriter?
> The planets closest to the Sun are Mercury, Mars, and Earth.

Ethnic and Religious References

Terms that relate to a particular culture, language, or race are capitalized.

> In Hawaii, Asian and Western cultures merge.
> Both English and Hebrew are spoken by Jews in Israel.
> African Americans and Latinos turned out to support their candidates.

Note: Hyphenate terms such as *African-American* and *French-Canadian* when they are used as adjectives (*African-American collection* or *French-Canadian citizens*). Do not hyphenate these terms when they are nouns.

Numbered and Lettered Items

Capitalize nouns followed by numbers or letters except in *page, paragraph, line, size,* and *verse* references.

Gate 15, Flight 1679	IRS Form 1040	Building A-31
Invoice No. 1314	Volume I, Appendix B	Medicare Form 23B
page 4, line 10	Interstate 85	Supplement No. 2
Model X-5498	size 7	No. 10 envelope
Extension 2306	Check No. 2445	verse 156

You are now ready to complete the reinforcement exercises.

HOTLINE QUERIES

Q: I don't know how to describe the copies made from our copy machine. Should I call them *Xerox* copies or something else?

A: They are *Xerox* copies only if made on a Xerox copier. Copies made on other brands of copy machines may be called *xerographic copies, machine copies, photocopies,* or just *copies.*

Q: In the doctor's office where I work, I see the word *medicine* capitalized, as in *the field of Medicine.* **Is this correct?**

A: No. General references should not be capitalized. Likewise, you would write *I plan to major in medicine* or *I plan to go to medical school.* If it were part of a title, as in the Northwestern College of *Medicine,* it would be capitalized.

Q: I work for the National Therapy Association. When I talk about *the association* in a letter, should I capitalize it?

A: No. When a shortened form of an organization name is used alone, it is generally not capitalized. In formal or legal documents (contracts, bylaws, printed announcements), it may be capitalized.

Q: I work for a state agency, and I'm not sure what to capitalize or hyphenate in this sentence: *State agencies must make forms available to non-English speaking applicants.***

A: Words with the prefix *non* are usually not hyphenated (*nonexistent, nontoxic*). But when *non* is joined to a word that must be capitalized, it is followed by a hyphen. Because the word *speaking* combines with *English* to form a single-unit adjective, it should be hyphenated. Thus, the expression should be typed *non-English-speaking applicants.*

Q: When we use a person's title, such as *business manager,* in place of a person's name,

shouldn't the title always be capitalized?

A: No. Business titles are capitalized only when they precede an individual's name, as in *Business Manager Smith.* Do not capitalize titles when they replace an individual's name: *Our business manager will direct the transaction.*

Q: I'm having trouble not capitalizing *president* when it refers to the president of the United States. It used to be capitalized. Why isn't it now?

A: For some time the trend has been away from "upstyle" capitalization. Fewer words are capitalized. Two principal authorities (*Merriam Webster Collegiate Dictionary* and *The Chicago Manual of Style*) both recommend lowercase for *president of the United States.* However, other authorities maintain that the term should always be capitalized because of the high regard for the office.

Q: Should the words *Internet* and *World Wide Web* be capitalized?

A: The *Internet* and the *World Wide Web* are currently considered proper nouns because these words represent specific places. They should, therefore, be capitalized. Likewise, the word *Web* should be capitalized when you are using it to refer specifically to the *World Wide Web.* We may see this change as more internets and webs are developed. For example, many companies have their own *intranets*. The word *intranet* is, therefore, not capitalized because it is considered a common noun.

Q: **What is the order of college degrees, and which ones are capitalized?**

A: Two kinds of undergraduate degrees are commonly awarded: the associate's degree, a two-year degree; and the bachelor's degree, a four-year degree. A variety of graduate degrees exist. The most frequently awarded are the master's degree and the doctorate. Merriam-Webster dictionaries do not capitalize the names of degrees: associate in arts degree, bachelor of science, master of arts, doctor of philosophy. Also notice the different prepositions that are used with these degrees. If you write these degrees as individual words, be sure to make them possessive (*associate's degree, bachelor's degree, master's degree*) However, when used with an individual's name, the abbreviations for degrees are capitalized (Bruce Gourlay, M.A.; Rhianna Landini, Ph.D.).

Q: **I'm writing a paper for my biology class on *in vitro fertilization*. Since this is a medical term, shouldn't I capitalize it?**

A: Don't capitalize medical procedures unless they are named after individuals (*Heimlich maneuver*). *In vitro* means "outside the living body." Specialists in the field use the abbreviation *IVF* after the first introduction of the term.

Q: **We're having an argument in our office about abbreviations. Can *department* be abbreviated *dep't?* How about *manufacturing* as *mf'g?* Where could we find a correct list of such abbreviations?**

A: In informal writing or when space is limited, words may be contracted or abbreviated. If a conventional abbreviation for a word exists, use it instead of a contracted form. Abbreviations are simpler to write and easier to read. For example, use *dept.* instead of *dep't;* use *natl.* instead of *nat'l;* use *cont.* instead of *cont'd.* Other accepted abbreviations are *ins.* for *insurance; mfg.* for *manufacturing; mgr.* for *manager;* and *mdse.* for *merchandise.* Notice that all abbreviations end with periods. Some dictionaries show abbreviations of words along with their definitions. Other dictionaries alphabetize abbreviations within the main entries, so that a reader must know how to spell an abbreviation to be able to locate it. Reference manuals often have lists of abbreviations that are very helpful.

InfoTrac Activity

InfoTrac in Action

As you begin to think about applying for a job, you want more information about cover letters and résumés.  Using an InfoTrac keyword search, find an article titled "DePaul Career Experts Offer Advice for Making Résumés, Cover Letters Stand Out in Tough Job Market." In the space provided or in a memo to your instructor, describe three important recommendations given for preparing résumés and cover letters.

_____

_____

_____

_____

_____

_____

_____

_____

_____

_____

15

NUMBERS

OBJECTIVES

When you have completed the material in this chapter, you will be able to do the following:

- Correctly choose between figure and word forms to express general numbers, and numbers beginning sentences.
- Form compound numbers correctly.
- Express monetary amounts, dates, clock time, addresses, and telephone and fax numbers appropriately.
- Use the correct form in writing related numbers, consecutive numbers, periods of time, and ages and anniversaries.
- Use the correct form in expressing numbers used with words, abbreviations, and symbols.
- Express correctly round numbers, weights, measurements, and fractions.
- Use the correct form in expressing percentages, decimals, and ordinals.

Just as capitalization is governed by convention, so is the expression of numbers. Usage and custom determine whether numbers are to be expressed in the form of a figure (for example, *5*) or in the form of a word (for example, *five*). Numbers expressed as figures are shorter and more easily comprehended, yet numbers used as words are necessary in certain instances. The following guidelines are observed in expressing numbers that appear in written *sentences*. Numbers that appear in business documents such as invoices, statements, and purchase orders are always expressed as figures.

GUIDELINES FOR EXPRESSING NUMBERS

General Rules

The basic rules for number express involve figure versus word form, numbers that begin sentences, and forming compound numbers

STUDY TIP

To remember it better, some people call this the "Rule of Ten": Words for one through ten; figures for 11 and above.

- ***Number versus figure form.*** The numbers *one* through *ten* are generally written as words. Numbers above *ten* are written as figures.

  > The committee consisted of *nine* regular members and *one* chair.
  > Online courses are offered by over *144* institutions in all *50* states.

- ***Numbers that begin sentences.*** Numbers that begin sentences are written as words. If a number involves more than two words, however, the sentence should be rewritten so that the number no longer falls at the beginning.

Thirty-four people applied for the Web designer position.
A total of *320* distributors agreed to market the product. (Not *Three hundred twenty* distributors agreed to market the product.)

■ *Forming compound numbers.* Compound numbers from *21* through *99* are hyphenated when they are written in word form.

Eighty-nine people applied for the office manager position.
Fifty-six stocks performed below expectations last month.

Money

Sums of money $1 or greater are expressed as figures. If a sum is a whole dollar amount, most business writers omit the decimal and zeros (even if the amount appears with fractional dollar amounts). Do not use a space between the currency symbol and the figure.

Although she budgeted only *$200,* Andrea spent *$234.50* for the scanner.
Our monthly statement showed purchases of *$7.13, $10, $43.50, $90,* and *$262.78.*

Sums less than $1 are written as figures that are followed by the word *cents.* If they are part of sums greater than $1, use a dollar sign and a decimal instead of the word *cents.*

Jack found that he had only *65 cents* with him.
Supplies for the project were listed at *$1.35, $.99, $2.80, $1,* and *$.40.*

Dates

In dates, numbers that appear after the name of the month are written in cardinal figures (*1, 2, 3,* etc.). Those that stand alone or appear before the name of a month are written in ordinal figures (*1st, 2nd, 3rd,* etc.).

The meeting is scheduled for *October 5* in our office.
On the *3rd* of April we opened a branch in Charleston.
The contract was signed on the 28th of November.

Most American business communicators express dates in the following form: month, day, year. An alternative form, used primarily in military and international correspondence, begins with the day of the month. Some business organizations prefer the international date style for its clarity, since it separates the numerical date of the month from the year.

By *October 1, 2006,* all construction on the annex must be completed. (General date format)
Our lease expires on *31 July 2007.* (Military and international format)

Clock Time

Figures are used when clock time is expressed with *a.m.* or *p.m.* Omit the colon and zeros with whole hours. When exact clock time is expressed with *o'clock,* either figures or words may be used. Note that phrases such as "in the afternoon" or "in the morning" may follow clock time expressed with *o'clock* but not with time expressed with *a.m.* and *p.m.*

The first shift starts at *8 a.m.,* and the second begins at *3:30 p.m.*
Department mail is usually distributed at *ten* (or *10*) *o'clock.*

Addresses

Except for the number *One,* house numbers are expressed as figures.

805 Sierra Drive   27321 Van Ness Avenue

One Wilshire Plaza   1762 Peachtree Street

Street names that involve the number *ten* or a lower number are written entirely as words. In street names involving numbers greater than *ten,* the numeral portion is written in figures. If no compass direction (*North, South, East, West*) separates a house number from a street number, the street number is expressed in ordinal form (*-st, -d, -th*).

201 Third Street
958 Eighth Avenue
201 West 53 Street
3261 South 105 Avenue
901 34th Avenue (Use *th* when no compass direction separates house number and numerical portion of street name.)

Telephone and Fax Numbers

Telephone and fax numbers are expressed with figures. When used, the area code is placed in parentheses preceding the telephone number. As an alternate form, you may separate the area code from the telephone number with a hyphen. A format that is emerging is to separate the parts of the number with periods.

Please call us at *555-1101* for further information.
You may reach me at *(801) 643-3267, Ext. 244,* after 9:30 a.m.
Orders faxed to us at *(415) 392-2194* will be processed immediately.
Call our toll-free number at *800-340-3281* for the latest sports updates.
You can place an order by calling us at *800.937.5594.*

Related Numbers

Numbers used similarly in the same document are considered related and should be expressed as the largest number is expressed. Thus, if the largest number is greater than *ten,* all the numbers should be expressed as figures.

On Monday *four* orders were placed, on Tuesday *eight* orders were placed, and on Wednesday an additional *nine* orders were placed.
Only *3* companies out of *147* failed to return the survey form.
Of the *46* jobs in the print queue, only *4* reports and *3* letters printed.
Nearly *20* employees will be expected to share the *15* computers, *8* printers, and *3* fax machines. (Note that items appearing in a series are always considered to be related.)

Unrelated numbers within the same reference are written as words or figures according to the general guidelines presented earlier in this chapter.

Two proposals covered *22* employees working in *three* branch offices.
During the *four* peak traffic hours, *three* bridges carry at least *20,000* cars.

Consecutive Numbers

When two numbers appear consecutively and both modify a following noun (such as *ten 37-cent stamps*), generally express the first number in words and the second in figures. If, however, the first number cannot be expressed in one or two

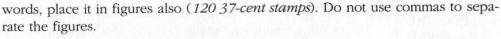

words, place it in figures also (*120 37-cent stamps*). Do not use commas to separate the figures.

> Historians divided the era into *four 25-year* periods. (Use word form for the first number and figure form for the second.)
>
> We ordered *ten 30-page* color brochures. (Use word form for the first number and figure form for the second.)
>
> Did you request *twenty 100-watt* bulbs? (Use word form for the first number and figure form for the second.)
>
> We'll need at least *150 100-watt* bulbs. (Use figure form for the first number since it requires more than two words.)

Periods of Time

Periods of time (seconds, minutes, hours, days, weeks, months, and years) are treated as any other general number. That is, numbers ten and below are written in word form. Numbers above ten are written in figure form.

> She hopes to find a new job in the next *three to five days*.
>
> Congress has regulated minimum wages for over *65 years*.
>
> The trial period for the software is *15 days*.
>
> After a *183-day* strike, workers returned to their jobs.

Figures are used to achieve special emphasis in expressing business concepts such as discount rates, interest rates, warranty periods, credit terms, loan periods, and payment terms.

> You earn a *2 percent* discount if your bill is paid within *10 days* of purchase.
>
> High interest rates are offered even on *6-* and *9-month* certificates of deposit.
>
> Your loan must be repaid within *60 days* in accordance with its terms.

Ages and Anniversaries

Ages and anniversaries that can be expressed in one or two words are generally written in word form. Those that require more than two words are written in figures. Figures are also used when an age (a) appears immediately after a name, (b) is expressed in exact years and months, or (c) is used in a legal or technical sense. Remember to hyphenate any compound ages between twenty-one and ninety-nine that are written in word form.

> When he was *forty-one*, Armistead Maupin became the company's president. (Use word form for age expressed in two or fewer words.)
>
> This year marks the *thirty-fifth* anniversary of the company's founding. (Use word form for anniversary expressed in two or fewer words.)
>
> Katharine Ralph, *63*, plans to retire in two years. (Use figure form for age appearing immediately after name.)
>
> The child was adopted when he was *3 years* and *8 months* old. (Use figure form for age expressed in terms of exact years and months.)
>
> Although the legal voting age is *18*, young people must be *21* to purchase alcohol. (Use figure form for age used in a legal sense.)

Numbers Used With Words, Abbreviations, and Symbols

Numbers used with words are expressed as figures.

page 6	Policy 651040	Area Code 925
Room 232	Volume 7	Section 8
Option 2	Form 1040	Assembly Bill 109

Numbers used with abbreviations are expressed as figures.

Apt. 19	Serial No. 2198675	Nos. 203 and 301
Ext. 167	Account No. 08166-05741	Social Security No. 250-93-6749

Notice that the word *number* is capitalized and abbreviated (*No.* or *Nos.*) when it precedes a number. Notice, too, that no commas are used in serial, account, and policy numbers.

Symbols (such as #, %, ¢) are usually avoided in contextual business writing (sentences). In other business documents where space is limited, however, symbols are frequently used. Numbers appearing with symbols are expressed as figures.

50%	34¢	#2 can	2/10, n/60

Round Numbers

Round numbers are approximations. They may be expressed in word or figure form, although figure form is shorter and easier to comprehend.

> Almost *400* (or *four hundred*) employees signed the petition.
> At last count we had received about *20* (or *twenty*) reservations.

For ease of reading, round numbers in the millions or billions should be expressed with a combination of figures and words.*

> The president asked for a budget cut of *$8.6 billion.*
> The world population has reached *6 billion.*
> Nearly *1.5 million* imported cars were sold this year.

ADDITIONAL GUIDELINES FOR EXPRESSING NUMBERS

Weights and Measurements

Weights and measurements are expressed as figures.

> A typical index card measures *3 by 5 inches.*
> Our specifications show the weight of the laptop to be *7 pounds 9 ounces.*
> The truck required *21 gallons* of gasoline and *2 quarts* of oil to travel *250 miles.*

In sentences the nouns following weights and measurements should be spelled out (for example, *21 gallons* instead of *21 gal.*). In business forms or in statistical presentations, however, such nouns may be abbreviated.

5″ × 17″	#10	16 oz.	20 sq. yds.	4 lb.	3 qt.

Fractions

Simple fractions are expressed as words. If a fraction functions as a noun, no hyphen is used. If it functions as an adjective, a hyphen separates its parts.

> Linguists predict that as many as *one half* of the world's 6,800 languages could disappear over the next century. (Fraction used as a noun)
> A *two-thirds* majority is needed to carry the measure. (Fraction used as an adjective)

---

*Note that only when *one million* is used as an approximation is it generally written in word form; otherwise, it is written *1 million.*

Complex fractions appearing in sentences may be written either as figures or as a combination of figures and words.

> The computer will execute a command in *1 millionth* of a second. (A combination of words and figures is easier to comprehend.)
> Flight records revealed that the emergency system was activated *13/200* of a second after the pilot was notified. (Figure form is easier to comprehend.)

Mixed fractions (whole numbers with fractions) are always expressed as figures. Use the extended character set of your word processing program to insert fractions that are written in figures. Fractions written in figures that are not found in extended character sets of word processing programs are formed by using the diagonal to separate the two parts. When fractions that are constructed with diagonals appear with key fractions, be consistent by using the diagonal construction for all the fractions involved.

> Office desks are expected to be *35¼* inches long, not *35½* inches. (Notice that no space follows a whole number and a key fraction.)
> The shelves were ordered to be *36 5/8* inches wide, not *36 3/8* inches. (Notice that fractions that must be constructed with slashes are separated from their related whole numbers.)

Percentages and Decimals

Percentages are expressed with figures followed by the word *percent*. The percent sign (%) is used only on business forms or in statistical presentations.

> Interest rates have been as low as *5½ percent* and as high as *19 percent*.
> Union leaders report that *52 percent* of all workers joined the union.

Decimals are expressed with figures. If a decimal does not contain a whole number (an integer) and does not begin with a zero, a zero should be placed before the decimal.

> Daryl Thomas set a record when he ran the race in *9.86* seconds. (Contains a whole number)
> Close examination revealed the settings to be *.005* inch off. (Begins with a zero)
> Less than *0.1* percent of the costs will be passed on to consumers. (Zero placed before decimal that neither contains a whole number nor begins with a zero)

Ordinals

Although ordinal numbers are generally expressed in word form (*first, second, third,* etc.), three exceptions should be noted: (a) figure form is used for dates appearing before a month or appearing alone, (b) figure form is used for street names involving numbers greater than *ten,* and (c) figure form is used when the ordinal would require more than two words.

- **Most ordinals**

> The company is celebrating its *fortieth anniversary.*
> Before the *twentieth century,* child labor laws were almost nonexistent.
> Of 237 sales representatives, Joanna ranked *second* in total sales.
> Paul Guerrero represents the *Twenty-ninth Congressional District.*

- **Dates**

> Your payment must be received by the *30th* to qualify for the cash discount.
> On the *2nd of June* we will begin construction.

■ *Streets*

> Traffic lights installed on *Second Street* have improved pedestrian safety.
> Our Customer Service Division has moved to *35th Street*.

■ *Larger ordinals.*

> First Federal Bank ranks *103rd* in terms of capital investments.

Some word processing programs automatically make superscripts from ordinals. If you dislike this program feature, you may turn it off.

You are now ready to complete the reinforcement exercises.

HOTLINE QUERIES

Q: **I recently saw the following format used by a business to publish its telephone number on its stationery and business cards: 512.582.0903. Is it now an option to use periods in telephone numbers?**

A: Using periods in telephone numbers is an emerging format, particularly in graphics design and Web design. It seems to be a stylistic affectation, perhaps reflecting European influences. To some, the style is upscale and chic; to others, it's just confusing. Telephone numbers written in the traditional formats are most readily recognized. That's why it's safe to stick with hyphens or parentheses: 512-582-0903 or (513) 582-0903.

Q: **I'm never sure when to hyphenate numbers, such as *thirty-one*. Is there some rule to follow?**

A: When written in word form, the numbers *twenty-one* through *ninety-nine* are hyphenated. Numbers are also hyphenated when they form compound adjectives and precede nouns (*ten-year-old* child, *16-story* building, *four-year* term, *30-day* lease).

Q: **My manager is preparing an advertisement for a charity event. She has written this: *Donors who give $100 dollars or more receive plaques.* I know this is not right, but I can't exactly put my finger on the problem**.

A: The problem is in *$100 dollars*. That is like saying *dollars dollars*. Drop the word *dollars* and use only the dollar sign: *Donors who give $100 or more . . . .*

Q: **I've always been confused by *imply* and *infer*. Which is correct in this sentence: *We (imply or infer) from your letter that the goods are lost.***

A: In your sentence use *infer*. *Imply* means "to state indirectly." *Infer* means "to draw a conclusion" or "to make a deduction based on facts." A listener or reader *infers*. A speaker or writer *implies*.

Q: **When fractions are written as words, why are they hyphenated sometimes and not hyphenated other times?**

A: Most writers do not hyphenate a fraction when it functions as a noun (*one fourth of the letters*).

When a fraction functions as an adjective, it is hyphenated (*a one-third gain in profits*).

Q: **Should I put quotation marks around figures to emphasize them? For example, *Your account has a balance of "$2,136.18."***

A: Certainly not! Quotation marks are properly used to indicate an exact quotation, or they may be used to enclose the definition of a word. They should not be used as a mechanical device for added emphasis.

Q: **I'm an engineer, and we have just had a discussion in our office concerning spelling. I have checked the dictionary, and it shows *usage*. Isn't this word ever spelled *useage?***

A: No. The only spelling of *usage* is without the internal *e*. You are probably thinking of the word *usable*, which does have a variant spelling—*useable*. Both forms are correct, but *usable* is recommended for its simplicity. Incidentally, if the word *usage* can be replaced by the word *use*, the latter is preferred (*the use* [not *usage*] *of ink pens is declining*).

Q: **How should I spell the word *lose* in this sentence? *The employee tripped over a (lose or loose) cord.***

A: In your sentence use the adjective *loose*, which means "not fastened," "not tight," or "having freedom of movement."

16

EFFECTIVE SENTENCES

OBJECTIVES

When you have completed the material in this chapter, you will be able to do the following:

- Eliminate wordy phrases and redundant words.
- Use the active voice in writing efficient sentences.
- Compose unified sentences by avoiding excessive detail and extraneous ideas.
- Write clear sentences using parallel construction for similar ideas.
- Place words, phrases, and clauses close to the words they modify.
- Avoid ambiguous pronoun references such as *this, that,* and *which.*

Business and professional people value efficient, economical writing that is meaningful and coherent. Wordy communication wastes the reader's time; unclear messages confuse the reader and are counterproductive. In the business world, where time is valuable, efficient writing is demanded. You can improve your writing skills by emulating the practices of good writers. Most good writers begin with a rough draft that they revise to produce a final version. This chapter shows you how to revise your rough draft sentences to make them more efficient, clear, emphatic, and coherent.

WRITING EFFICIENT SENTENCES

To write efficiently, you must be able to write concisely. Following are techniques for expressing your sentences in as few words as possible

Revising Wordy Phrases

Sentences are efficient when they convey a thought directly and economically—that is, in the fewest possible words. Good writers remove all useless verbiage from their writing. Some of the most common and comfortable phrases are actually full of "word fat"; when examined carefully, these phrases can be pared down considerably.

WORDY PHRASES	CONCISE SUBSTITUTES
as per your suggestion	as you suggested
at the present time	now
at this point in time	now
due to the fact that	because
for the purpose of	to
give consideration to	consider
in addition to the above	also

SPOT THE BLOOPER

In *Skyway News/Freeway News,* describing a restaurant in Mantonville, Minnesota: "Proprietor Paul J. Pappas extends his hostility to tour groups. Call for reservations."

SPOT THE BLOOPER

U.S. Senate candidate Ben Nelson, of Nebraska, sent a solicitation letter promising to "vote my conscious."

WORDY PHRASES	CONCISE SUBSTITUTES
in all probability	probably
in connection with	for
in spite of the fact that	even though
in the amount of	for
in the event that	if
in the near future	soon
in the neighborhood of	about
in view of the fact that	since
it is recommended that	we suggest that
under date of	on, dated
until such time as	until
with regard to	about

Notice that the revised versions of the following wordy sentences are more efficient:

WORDY: *As per your suggestion,* we will change the meeting.
MORE EFFICIENT: *As you suggested,* we will change the meeting.

WORDY: *Until such time as* we receive the contract, we cannot proceed.
MORE EFFICIENT: *When* we receive the contract, we can proceed.

WORDY: Bob Eddy will *in all probability* run for reelection.
MORE EFFICIENT: Bob Eddy will *probably* run for reelection.

Eliminating Redundant Words

Words that are needlessly repetitive are said to be "redundant." Business writers can achieve greater efficiency (and thus more effective sentences) by eliminating redundant words or phrases, such as the following:

advance warning	exactly identical	perfectly clear
alter or change	few in number	personal opinion
assemble together	free and clear	potential opportunity
basic fundamentals	grateful thanks	positively certain
collect together	great majority	proposed plan
consensus of opinion	integral part	reason why
contributing factor	last and final	refer back
dollar amount	midway between	true facts
each and every	new changes	very unique
end result	past history	visible to the eye

REDUNDANT: Have you *assembled together* the new bookshelves?
MORE EFFICIENT: Have you *assembled* the new bookshelves?

REDUNDANT: This paragraph is *exactly identical* to that one.
MORE EFFICIENT: This paragraph is *identical* to that one.

REDUNDANT: *First and foremost,* we must balance the budget.
MORE EFFICIENT: *First,* we must balance the budget.

REDUNDANT: The *reason why* we are discussing the issue is to try to reach a *consensus of opinion*.
MORE EFFICIENT: The *reason* we are discussing the issue it to try to reach a *consensus*.

Using Active Voice

Sentences that use active verbs are more economical—and, of course, more direct—than those using passive verbs.

PASSIVE:	A discrepancy in the bank balance *was detected by auditors*.
ACTIVE:	*Auditors detected* a discrepancy in the bank balance.
PASSIVE:	In the April issue your article *will be published by us*.
ACTIVE:	In the April issue *we will publish* your article.
PASSIVE:	The CEO *was informed by the vice president* that the merger fell through.
MORE EFFICIENT:	The *vice president informed* the CEO that the merger fell through.

WRITING CLEAR SENTENCES

Clear sentences are those that immediately convey their central thought. Good writers achieve sentence clarity by developing unified sentences, using parallel construction, avoiding misplaced modifiers, and using unambiguous pronoun references.

Writing Unified Sentences

A sentence is unified if it contains only closely related ideas. When extraneous or unrelated ideas appear in a sentence, they confuse the reader. Sentences lacking unity can be improved by removing the extraneous ideas or by shifting the unrelated ideas to separate sentences.

LACKS UNITY:	I am appreciative of the time you spent interviewing me last week, and I plan to enroll in an Internet research course immediately.
IMPROVED:	I appreciate the time you spent with me last week. Because of our interview, I plan to enroll in an Internet research course immediately.
LACKS UNITY:	It is easy for you to do your holiday shopping, and we offer three unique catalogs.
IMPROVED:	Because we offer three unique catalogs, it is easy for you to do your holiday shopping.
LACKS UNITY:	Last spring the Treasury Department asked Americans to circulate pennies, and many people toss these coins in a junk drawer or hoard them in mayonnaise jars, creating a shortage, and some people just throw them away.
IMPROVED:	Last spring the Treasury Department asked Americans to circulate pennies. Many people toss these coins in junk drawers or hoard them in mayonnaise jars. Some people even throw them away, thus creating a shortage.

The inclusion of excessive detail can also damage sentence unity. If many details are necessary for overall clarity, put them in additional sentences.

EXCESSIVE DETAIL:	Germany is preparing to auction 20 castles that formerly belonged to the Communist government, although hundreds of bidders have submitted offers and price is not the determining factor because the government is looking for

From *The Northern Star,* student newspaper of Northern Illinois University: "Never pet, play with, or give commands to a person using a guide dog without permission."

SPOT THE BLOOPER

From a job applicant's cover letter: "I've updated my résumé so it's more appalling to employers."

Sign in a souvenir shop in York Beach, Maine: "You brake it, you pay for it."

responsible investors who can protect the cultural values of the monuments as well as preserve their structures.

IMPROVED: Germany will auction 20 castles that formerly belonged to the Communist government. Price is not as important as finding responsible investors who can protect and preserve the monuments.

EXCESSIVE DETAIL: A report can be important, but it may not be effective or be read because it is too long and bulky, which will also make it more difficult to distribute, to store, and to handle, as well as increasing its overall cost.

IMPROVED: An important report may be ineffective because it is too long. Its bulk may increase its costs and make it difficult to read, handle, distribute, and store.

Developing Parallel Construction

Sentence clarity can be improved by expressing similar ideas with similar grammatical structures. For example, if you are listing three ideas, do not use *ing* words for two of the ideas and a *to* verb for the third idea: *buying, trading, and selling* (not *to sell*). Use nouns with nouns, verbs with verbs, phrases with phrases, and clauses with clauses. In the following list, use all verbs: *the machine sorted, stamped, and counted* (not *and had a counter*). For phrases, the wording for all parts of the list should be matched: *Stopping distances were checked on concrete pavement, over winding roads, and on wet surfaces* (not *when it rains*).

FAULTY: Improving the stability of the car resulted in less passenger comfort, reduced visibility, and the car weighed more.

IMPROVED: Improving the stability of the car resulted in less passenger comfort, reduced visibility, and added weight. (Matches nouns)

FAULTY: The new T-1 line helped us improve quality, save money, and we got our work done faster.

IMPROVED: The new T-1 helped us improve quality, save money, and work faster. (Matches verb-noun construction)

FAULTY: Collecting, organizing, and documentation—these are important steps in researching a problem.

IMPROVED: Collecting, organizing, and documenting—these are important steps in researching a problem. (Matches *ing* nouns)

Avoiding Misplaced Modifiers

As you will recall, modifiers are words, phrases, or clauses that limit or restrict other words, phrases, or clauses. To be clear, modifiers must be placed carefully so that the words they modify are obvious. When a modifier is placed so that it does not appear to be modifying the word or words intended to be modified, that modifier is said to be *misplaced*. In Chapter 6 introductory verbal modifiers were discussed. An introductory verbal modifier is sometimes misplaced simply by being at the beginning of the sentence. Consider how the introductory verbal modifier makes the following sentence nonsensical: *While pumping gas, an unoccupied car rolled into mine.* After all, the unoccupied car is not pumping gas. In positions other than the beginning of the sentence, misplaced modifiers may also damage sentence clarity.

FAULTY:	Please take time to examine the brochure *that is enclosed with your family.*
IMPROVED:	Please take time to examine *with your family* the enclosed brochure.
FAULTY:	We provide a map for all *visitors reduced to a 1-inch scale.*
IMPROVED:	For all visitors we provide a *map reduced to a 1-inch scale.*
FAULTY:	A 30-year-old St. Petersburg man *was found murdered by his parents* in his home late Tuesday.
IMPROVED:	Murdered in his home, a 30-year-old St. Petersburg man *was found by his parents* late Tuesday.

Improving Pronoun References

Sentence confusion results from the use of pronouns without clear antecedents. Be particularly careful with the pronouns *this, that, which,* and *it.* Confusion often results when these pronouns have as their antecedents an entire clause. Such confusion can usually be avoided by substituting a noun for the pronoun or by following the pronoun with a clarifying noun (or nouns).

FAULTY:	Members of the European Union want to prevent makers of food, wine, and spirits from calling products by regional names unless they were produced in those regions. *They* are targeting many items that most Americans consider generic, such as balsamic vinegar, bologna, mozzarella, and Chianti.
IMPROVED:	Members of the European Union want to prevent makers of food, wine, and spirits from calling products by regional names unless they were produced in those regions. *EU members* are targeting many items that most Americans consider generic, such as balsamic vinegar, bologna, mozzarella, and Chianti.
FAULTY:	We have a policy of responding to customer inquiries and orders on the day they are received. *That* keeps us busy and keeps our customers satisfied.
IMPROVED:	We have a policy of responding to customer inquiries and orders on the day they are received. *That policy* keeps us busy and keeps our customers satisfied.
FAULTY:	Our government contracts require work on hundreds of projects that demand constant updating and access to technical data, supplies, and references, *which* explains why an open office design allowing team interaction is necessary.
IMPROVED:	Our government contracts require work on hundreds of projects that demand constant updating and access to technical data, supplies, and references. *These needs* explain why an open office design allowing team interaction is essential.

You are now ready to complete the reinforcement exercises.

Q: I just typed this sentence: *You will see in our manual where multiple bids must be obtained.* Somewhere from my distant past I seem to recall that *where* should not be used in this way. Can you help me?

A: You're right. *Where* should not be substituted for the relative pronoun *that.* In your sentence, use *that.* A similar faulty construction to be avoided is the use of *while* for *although* (*although* [not *while*] *I agree with his position, I disagree with his procedures*).

Q: In my writing I want to use *firstly* and *secondly.* Are they acceptable?

A: Both words are acceptable, but most good writers prefer *first* and *second,* because they are more efficient and equally accurate.

Q: How do you spell *marshal,* as used in *the Grand Marshal of the Rose Parade?*

A: The preferred spelling is with a single *l: marshal.* In addition to describing an individual who directs a ceremony, the noun *marshal* refers to a high military officer or a city law officer who carries out court orders (*the marshal served papers on the defendant*). As a verb, *marshal* means "to bring together" or "to order in an effective way" (*the attorney marshaled convincing arguments*). The similar-sounding word *martial* is an adjective and means "warlike" or "military" (*martial law was declared after the riot*).

Q: In a business report is it acceptable to write the following? *Most everyone agrees . . . .*

A: In this construction *most* is a shortened form of *almost.* Although such constructions are heard in informal speech, they should not appear in business writing. Instead, use the longer form: *Almost everyone agrees . . . .*

Q: Everyone says "consensus of opinion." Yet, I understand that there is some objection to this expression.

A: Yes, the expression is widely used. However, since *consensus* means "collective opinion," the addition of the word *opinion* results in a redundancy.

Q: My boss wrote a report with this sentence: *Saleswise, our staff is excellent.* Should I change it?

A: Never change wording without checking with the author. You might point out, however, that the practice of attaching *-wise* to nouns is frowned on by many language experts. Such combinations as *budgetwise, taxwise,* and *productionwise* are considered commercial jargon. Suggest this revision: *On the basis of sales, our staff is excellent.*

Q: This sentence doesn't sound right to me, but I can't decide how to improve it: *The reason I'm applying is because I enjoy editing.* Do you have any suggestions?

A: The problem lies in this construction: *the reason . . . is because . . . .* Only nouns or adjectives may act as complements following linking verbs. In your sentence an adverbial clause follows the linking verb and sounds awkward. One way to improve the sentence is to substitute a noun clause beginning with *that: The reason I'm applying is that I enjoy editing.* An even better way to improve the sentence would be to make it a direct statement: *I'm applying because I enjoy editing.*

Q: I received a magazine advertisement recently that promised me a *free gift* and a *15 percent off discount* if I subscribed. What's wrong with this wording?

A: You've got a double winner here in the category of redundancies. The word *gift* suggests *free;* therefore, to say *free gift* is like *saying I'm studying English English.* It would be better to say *special gift.* In the same way, *15 percent off discount* repeats itself. Omit *off.*

Q: Another employee and I are collaborating on a report. I wanted to write this: *Money*

was lost due to poor attendance. She says the sentence should read: *Money was lost because of poor attendance.* My version is more concise. Which of us is right?

A: Most language authorities agree with your coauthor. *Due to* is acceptable when it functions as an adjective, as in *Success was due to proper timing.* In this sense, *due to* is synonymous with *attributable to.* However, when *due to* functions as a preposition, as in your sentence, language experts find fault. Your friend is right; substitute *because of.*

Q: We have a new electronic mail system, and one of the functions is "messaging" people. When folks say, *I'll message you,* it really grates on my nerves. Is this correct?

A: "Messaging" is certainly a hot term with the explosion of e-mail. As to its correctness, we think we've caught language in the act of evolving. What's happened here is the reinstitution of a noun (*message*) as a verb. Converting nouns into verbs is common in English (he *cornered* the market, we *tabled* the motion, I *penciled* it in on my calendar, the farmer *trucked* the vegetables to market). Actually, *message* was sometimes used as a verb nearly a century ago (in 1896 *the bill was messaged over from the house*).

However, its recent use has been almost exclusively as a noun. Today, it is increasingly being used again as a verb. New uses of words usually become legitimate when the words fill a need and are immediately accepted. Some word uses, though, appear to be mere fads, like *The homeless child could not language* her fears. Forcing the noun *language* to function as a verb is unnecessary since a good word already exists for the purpose: *express*. But other "nouns-made-verbs" have been in use long enough to sound reasonable: I *faxed* the document, he *videotaped* the program, she *keyed* the report.

APPENDIX A
DEVELOPING SPELLING SKILLS

WHY IS ENGLISH SPELLING SO DIFFICULT?

No one would dispute the complaint that many English words are difficult to spell. Why is spelling in our language so perplexing? For one thing, our language has borrowed many of its words from other languages. English has a Germanic base on which a superstructure of words borrowed from French, Latin, Greek, and other languages of the world has been erected. For this reason, its words are not always formed by regular patterns of letter combinations. In addition, spelling is made difficult because the pronunciation of English words is constantly changing. Today's spelling was standardized nearly 300 years ago, but many words are pronounced differently today than they were then. Therefore, pronunciation often provides little help in spelling. Consider, for example, the words *sew* and *dough*.

WHAT CAN BE DONE TO IMPROVE ONE'S SPELLING?

Spelling is a skill that can be developed, just as arithmetic, keyboarding, and other skills can be developed. Because the ability to spell is a prerequisite for success in business and in most other activities, effort expended to acquire this skill is effort well spent.

Three traditional approaches to improving spelling have met with varying degrees of success.

1. Rules or Guidelines

The spelling of English words is consistent enough to justify the formulation of a few spelling rules, perhaps more appropriately called guidelines since the generalizations in question are not invariably applicable. Such guidelines are, in other words, helpful but not infallible.

2. Mnemonics

Another approach to improving one's ability to spell involves the use of mnemonics or memory devices. For example, the word *principle* might be associated with the word *rule*, to form in the mind of the speller a link between the meaning and the spelling of *principle*. To spell *capitol*, one might think of the *dome* of the capitol building and focus on the *o*'s in both words. The use of mnemonics can be an effective device for the improvement of spelling only if the speller makes a real effort to develop the necessary memory hooks.

3. Rote Learning

A third approach to the improvement of spelling centers on memorization. The word is studied by the speller until it can be readily reproduced in the mind's eye.

THE 1-2-3 SPELLING PLAN

Proficiency in spelling is not attained without concentrated effort. Here's a plan to follow in mastering the 400 commonly misspelled words included in this appendix. For each word, try this 1-2-3 approach.

1. Is a spelling guideline applicable? If so, select the appropriate guideline and study the word in relation to that guideline.
2. If no guideline applies, can a memory device be created to aid in the recall of the word?
3. If neither a guideline nor a memory device will work, the word must be memorized. Look at the word carefully. Pronounce it. Write it or repeat it until you can visualize all its letters in your mind's eye.

Before you try the 1-2-3 plan, become familiar with the six spelling guidelines that follow. These spelling guidelines are not intended to represent all the possible spelling rules appearing in the various available spelling books. These six guidelines are, however, among the most effective and helpful of the recognized spelling rules.

Guideline 1: Words Containing *ie* or *ei*

Although there are exceptions to it, the following familiar rhyme can be helpful.

Write *i* before *e*
Except after *c*,
Or when sounded like *a*
As in *neighbor* and *weigh*.

Study these words illustrating the three parts of the rhyme.

i BEFORE *e*		EXCEPT AFTER *c*	OR WHEN SOUNDED LIKE *a*
achieve	grief	ceiling	beige
belief	ingredient	conceive	eight
believe	mischief	deceive	freight
brief	niece	perceive	heir
cashier	piece	receipt	neighbor
chief	shield	receive	reign
convenient	sufficient		their
field	view		vein
friend	yield		weight

Exceptions: These exceptional *ei* and *ie* words must be learned by rote or with the use of a mnemonic device.

caffeine	height	seize
either	leisure	sheik
financier	neither	sleight
foreigner	protein	weird

Guideline 2: Words Ending in e

For most words ending in an *e*, the final *e* is dropped when the word is joined to a suffix beginning with a vowel (such as *ing, able,* or *al*). The final *e* is retained when a suffix beginning with a consonant (such as *ment, less, ly,* or *ful*) is joined to such a word.

Final *e* Dropped	Final *e* Retained
believe, believing	arrange, arrangement
care, caring	require, requirement
hope, hoping	hope, hopeless
receive, receiving	care, careless
desire, desirable	like, likely
cure, curable	approximate, approximately
move, movable	definite, definitely
value, valuable	sincere, sincerely
disperse, dispersal	use, useful
arrive, arrival	hope, hopeful

Exceptions: The few exceptions to this spelling guideline are among the most frequently misspelled words. As such, they deserve special attention. Notice that they all involve a dropped final *e.*

acknowledgment	ninth
argument	truly
judgment	wholly

Guideline 3: Words Ending in *ce* or *ge*

When *able* or *ous* is added to words ending in *ce* or *ge,* the final *e* is retained if the *c* or *g* is pronounced softly (as in *change* or *peace*).

advantage, advantageous	change, changeable
courage, courageous	service, serviceable
outrage, outrageous	manage, manageable

Guideline 4: Words Ending in *y*

Words ending in a *y* that is preceded by a consonant normally change the *y* to *i* before all suffixes except those beginning with an *i.*

Change *y* to *i* Because *y* Is Preceded by a Consonant	Do Not Change *y* to *i* Because *y* Is Preceded by a Vowel
accompany, accompaniment	employ, employer
study, studied, studious	annoy, annoying, annoyance
duty, dutiful	stay, staying, stayed
industry, industrious	attorney, attorneys
carry, carriage	valley, valleys
apply, appliance	
try, tried	Do Not Change *y* to *i* When Adding *ing*
empty, emptiness	accompany, accompanying
forty, fortieth	apply, applying
secretary, secretaries	study, studying
company, companies	satisfy, satisfying
hurry, hurries	try, trying

Exceptions: day, daily; dry, dried; mislay, mislaid; pay, paid; shy, shyly; gay, gaily

Guideline 5: Doubling a Final Consonant

If one-syllable words or two-syllable words accented on the second syllable end in a single consonant preceded by a single vowel, the final consonant is doubled before the addition of a suffix beginning with a vowel.

Although complex, this spelling guideline is extremely useful and therefore well worth mastering. Many spelling errors can be avoided by applying this guideline.

ONE-SYLLABLE WORDS	TWO-SYLLABLE WORDS
can, canned	acquit, acquitting, acquittal
drop, dropped	admit, admitted, admitting
fit, fitted	begin, beginner, beginning
get, getting	commit, committed, committing
man, manned	control, controller, controlling
plan, planned	defer, deferred (but deference*)
run, running	excel, excelled, excelling
shut, shutting	occur, occurrence, occurring
slip, slipped	prefer, preferring (but preference*)
swim, swimming	recur, recurred, recurrence
ton, tonnage	refer, referring (but reference*)

*Because the accent shifts to the first syllable, the final consonant is not doubled.

Here is a summary of conditions necessary for application of this guideline.

1. The word must end in a single consonant.
2. The final consonant must be preceded by a single vowel.
3. The word must be accented on the second syllable (if it has two syllables).

Words derived from *cancel, offer, differ, equal, suffer,* and *benefit* are not governed by this guideline because they are accented on the first syllable.

Guideline 6: Prefixes and Suffixes

For words in which the letter that ends the prefix is the same as the letter that begins the main word (such as in *dissimilar*), both letters must be included. For words in which a suffix begins with the same letter that ends the main word (such as in *coolly*), both letters must also be included.

PREFIX	MAIN WORD	MAIN WORD	SUFFIX
dis	satisfied	accidental	ly
ir	responsible	incidental	ly
il	literate	clean	ness
mis	spell	cool	ly
mis	state	even	ness
un	necessary	mean	ness

On the other hand, do not supply additional letters when adding prefixes to main words.

PREFIX	MAIN WORD
dis	appoint (*not* dissappoint)
dis	appearance
mis	take

Perhaps the most important guideline one can follow in spelling correctly is to use the dictionary whenever in doubt.

400 MOST FREQUENTLY MISSPELLED WORDS*
(DIVIDED INTO 20 LISTS OF 20 WORDS EACH)

List 1	List 2	List 3
1. absence	21. afraid	41. applying
2. acceptance	22. against	42. approaches
3. accessible	23. aggressive	43. appropriate
4. accidentally	24. all right	44. approximately
5. accommodate	25. a lot, allot	45. arguing
6. accompaniment	26. alphabetical	46. argument
7. accurately	27. already, all ready	47. arrangement
8. accustom	28. although	48. article
9. achievement	29. amateur	49. athlete
10. acknowledgment	30. among	50. attack
11. acquaintance	31. amount	51. attendance, attendants
12. acquire	32. analysis	52. attitude
13. across	33. analyze	53. attorneys
14. actually	34. angel, angle	54. auxiliary
15. adequately	35. annoyance	55. basically
16. admitted	36. annual	56. beautiful
17. adolescence	37. answer	57. before
18. advantageous	38. apologized	58. beginning
19. advertising	39. apparent	59. believing
20. advice, advise	40. appliance	60. benefited

List 4	List 5	List 6
61. biggest	81. companies	101. description
62. breath, breathe	82. competition	102. desirable
63. brief	83. completely	103. destroy
64. business	84. conceive	104. development
65. calendar	85. conscience	105. difference
66. capital, capitol	86. conscientious	106. dining, dinning
67. career	87. conscious	107. disappearance
68. careless	88. considerably	108. disappoint
69. carrying	89. consistent	109. disastrous
70. cashier	90. continuous	110. discipline
71. ceiling	91. controlling	111. discussion
72. certain	92. controversial	112. disease
73. challenge	93. convenience	113. dissatisfied
74. changeable	94. council, counsel	114. distinction
75. chief	95. cylinder	115. divide
76. choose, chose	96. daily	116. doesn't
77. cloths, clothes	97. deceive	117. dominant
78. column	98. decision	118. dropped
79. coming	99. define	119. due
80. committee	100. dependent	120. during

*Compiled from lists of words most frequently misspelled by students and businesspeople.

List 7	List 8	List 9
121. efficient	141. February	161. happiness
122. eligible	142. fictitious	162. harassment
123. embarrass	143. field	163. hear, here
124. enough	144. finally	164. height
125. entrepreneur	145. financially	165. heroes
126. environment	146. foreigner	166. hopeless
127. equipped	147. fortieth, forty	167. hoping
128. especially	148. fourth, forth	168. humorous
129. exaggerate	149. forward, foreword	169. hungry
130. excellence	150. freight	170. ignorance
131. except	151. friend	171. imaginary
132. exercise	152. fulfill	172. imagine
133. existence	153. fundamentally	173. immediately
134. experience	154. further, farther	174. immense
135. explanation	155. generally	175. importance
136. extremely	156. government	176. incidentally
137. familiar	157. governor	177. independent
138. families	158. grammar	178. indispensable
139. fascinate	159. grateful	179. industrious
140. favorite	160. guard	180. inevitable

List 10	List 11	List 12
181. influential	201. leisurely	221. mechanics
182. ingredient	202. library	222. medicine
183. initiative	203. license	223. medieval
184. intelligence	204. likely	224. mere
185. interest	205. literature	225. miniature
186. interference	206. lives	226. minutes
187. interpretation	207. loneliness	227. mischief
188. interrupt	208. loose, lose	228. misspell
189. involve	209. losing	229. mistake
190. irrelevant	210. luxury	230. muscle
191. irresponsible	211. magazine	231. mysterious
192. island	212. magnificence	232. naturally
193. jealous	213. maintenance	233. necessary
194. judgment	214. manageable	234. neighbor
195. kindergarten	215. maneuver	235. neither
196. knowledge	216. manner	236. nervous
197. laboratory	217. manufacturer	237. nickel
198. laborer	218. marriage	238. niece
199. laid	219. mathematics	239. ninety
200. led, lead	220. meant	240. ninth

List 13	List 14	List 15
241. noticeable	261. passed, past	281. possible
242. numerous	262. pastime	282. practical
243. obstacle	263. peaceable	283. precede
244. occasionally	264. peculiar	284. preferred
245. occurrence, occur	265. perceive	285. prejudice
246. off	266. performance	286. preparation
247. offered	267. permanent	287. prevalent
248. official	268. permitted	288. principal, principle
249. omitted	269. persistent	289. privilege
250. operate	270. personal, personnel	290. probably
251. opinion	271. persuading	291. proceed
252. opportunity	272. phase, faze	292. professor
253. opposite	273. philosophy	293. prominent
254. organization	274. physical	294. proving
255. origin	275. piece	295. psychology
256. original	276. planned	296. pursuing
257. paid	277. pleasant	297. quantity
258. pamphlet	278. poison	298. quiet, quite
259. parallel	279. political	299. really
260. particular	280. possession	300. receipt

List 16	List 17	List 18
301. receiving	321. satisfying	341. speak, speech
302. recognize	322. scenery	342. specimen
303. recommend	323. schedule	343. stationary, stationery
304. reference	324. science	344. stopped
305. referring, refer	325. secretaries	345. stories
306. regard	326. seize	346. straight, strait
307. relative	327. sense, since	347. strenuous
308. relieving	328. sentence	348. stretch
309. religious	329. separation	349. strict
310. reminiscent	330. sergeant	350. studying
311. repetition	331. serviceable	351. substantial
312. representative	332. several	352. subtle
313. requirement	333. shining	353. succeed
314. resistance	334. shoulder	354. success
315. responsible	335. significance	355. sufficient
316. restaurant	336. similar	356. summary
317. rhythm	337. simply	357. suppose
318. ridiculous	338. sincerely	358. surprise
319. sacrifice	339. site, cite, sight	359. suspense
320. safety	340. source	360. swimming

List 19	List 20
361. syllable	381. tremendous
362. symbol	382. tried
363. symmetrical	383. truly
364. synonymous	384. undoubtedly
365. technique	385. unnecessary
366. temperament	386. until
367. temperature	387. unusual
368. tendency	388. useful
369. than, then	389. using
370. their, there, they're	390. vacuum
371. themselves	391. valuable
372. theories	392. varies
373. therefore	393. vegetable
374. thorough	394. view
375. though	395. weather, whether
376. through	396. weird
377. together	397. were, where
378. tomorrow	398. wholly, holy
379. tragedies	399. writing
380. transferred	400. yield

APPENDIX B
ANSWERS TO ODD-NUMBERED REINFORCEMENT EXERCISES

CHAPTER 1

Exercise A

1. chiefs
3. companies
5. stockholders
7. viruses
9. 1990s

Exercise B

1. liabilities
3. franchises
5. mayors-elect
7. bills of lading
9. millennia (or millenniums)
11. databases
13. p's and q's
15. the Wolfs
17. 10s
19. IOUs
21. chefs
23. 2000s
25. Nos.
27. workmen
29. ports of entry

Exercise C

1. Kennedys
3. ratios
5. 1950s
7. pp.
9. CEOs
11. Sanchezes
13. co-owners
15. W-2s

Exercise D

1. is
3. were
5. Were
7. were
9. theses

CHAPTER 2

Exercise A

1. the alibi of the defendant; No
3. the uniforms of all players; Yes
5. research of four years; Yes
7. a
9. b

Exercise B

1. job applicant's qualifications
3. the company's policies
5. managers' meeting
7. ten months' interest
9. the patient's appointment

Exercise C

1. agencies'
3. inventor's
5. cents'
7. people's
9. Harrises'

Exercise D

1. years'
3. C
5. C
7. Disney's
9. investors'

Exercise E

1. light bulb filament (or filament of the light bulb)
3. CEO's
5. Human Resources
7. small claims
9. C

Exercise F

1. Chavez's or Chavez'
3. Kim's
5. Elvis's or Elvis'
7. boss's
9. yesterday's

CHAPTER 3

Exercise A

1. him
3. its
5. he
7. her and me
9. Who
11. Who's
13. We
15. he or she is
17. his or her
19. his

Exercise B

1. he
3. they
5. We
7. them
9. him

Exercise C

1. its
3. It's
5. she
7. him and her
9. she

Exercise D

1. *I* instead of *me*
3. *her and him* instead of *she and he*
5. *he* instead of *him*
7. *me* instead of *I*
9. *me* instead of *myself*

Exercise E

1. who
3. whom
5. whoever
7. who
9. whom

Exercise F

1. Who's
3. whose
5. Who's

Exercise G

1. their
3. his or her
5. his or her
7. his or her
9. its

Exercise H

Answers will vary.

1. a. All residents must display their parking permits.
   b. Every resident must display a parking permit.
   c. Every resident must display his or her parking permit.
3. a. Patients who don't accurately report their histories to their doctors run the risk of misdiagnosis.
   b. A patient who doesn't report an accurate history to a doctor runs the risk of misdiagnosis.
   c. A patient who doesn't accurately report his or her history to his or her doctor runs the risk of misdiagnosis.

Exercise I

1. *its* instead of *their*
3. *its* instead of *their*
5. *his or her* instead of *their*
7. C
9. *its* instead of *their*

CHAPTER 4

Exercise A

1. flown
3. shrank
5. began
7. seen
9. gave

Exercise B

1. L	7. A
3. A	9. A
5. A	

Exercise C

1. careful (linking verb is *are*)
3. comfortable (linking verb is *feels*)
5. she (linking verb is *was*)
7. upset (linking verb is *looked*)
9. they (linking verb is *was*)

Exercise D

1. active	7. passive
3. passive	9. passive
5. active	

Exercise E

1. shrunk	9. paid
3. choose	11. written
5. gone	13. brought
7. stolen	15. thrown

Exercise F

1. lie	7. lies
3. lying	9. laying
5. lay	

Exercise G

1. raise	7. raised
3. raise	9. rises
5. risen	

CHAPTER 5

Exercise A

1. is	9. Every one
3. are	11. were
5. is	13. are
7. are	15. are

Exercise B

1. is (subject is *degree*)
3. was (subject is *description*)
5. make (subject is *athletes*)

Exercise C

1. is	17. are
3. is	19. is
5. is	21. Is
7. were	23. is
9. is	25. supports
11. are	27. has
13. have	29. are
15. is	

CHAPTER 6

Exercise A

1. Rachel	7. his
3. His	9. Ratha's
5. Sonia's	

Exercise B

1. b
3. a
5. b
7. b
9. a

Exercise C

1. 1 (times,)	9. 1 (proprietor,)
3. 1 (news,)	11. 1 (messages,)
5. 0	13. 0
7. 1 (employees,)	15. 0

Exercise D

1. 2 (Galvin, project,)	7. 0
3. 2 (Despina, marketing,)	9. 0
5. 2 (Sole, daily,)	

Exercise E

1. 1 (hired,)	7. 1 (carefully,)
3. 2 (CEO, pressure,)	9. 1 (hazards,)
5. 2 (Motors, suppliers,)	

Exercise F

Answers will vary.

1. Running in the Boston Marathon, she made her dream come true.
3. To be binding, every contract must be supported by a consideration.
5. Locked securely in the vault, the documents were accessible only to Lily Zandi.
7. Noxious fumes coming from the nearby auto paint shop made many office workers sick.
9. Rick Risbrough found his wallet lying behind the counter.

CHAPTER 7

Exercise A

1. worst
3. this
5. better
7. day-to-day
9. more quickly
11. bad
13. calm
15. anything
17. year to year
19. any other city

Exercise B

1. These
3. best
5. easily
7. strongly
9. less
11. doesn't have any
13. more nearly accurate
15. has only one
17. most
19. any

Exercise C

1. a
3. an
5. a
7. an
9. an
11. an
13. an
15. an

Exercise D

1. a
3. b
5. a
7. b
9. a

Exercise E

1. no comma needed
3. concise, courteous
5. no comma needed

Exercise F

1. better
3. an
5. well
7. first two
9. any other investor
11. sold only
13. fewer
15. faster
17. bad
19. three- and four-bedroom

CHAPTER 8

Exercise A

1. should have
3. me
5. could have
7. as if
9. between
11. of
13. to stay
15. with
17. accept
19. to

Exercise B

1. *him* instead of *he*
3. *too early* instead of *to early*

5. *from* instead of *off of*
7. *her* instead of *she*
9. *different from* instead of *different than*
11. *differ with* instead of *differ from*
13. *besides* instead of *beside*
15. C
17. *contrasts with* instead of *contrasts to*
19. *adept in* instead of *adept at*

Exercise C

1. omit *from*
3. omit *to*
5. omit *at*
7. appreciation *for*
9. omit *of*

Exercise D

1. among
3. inside
5. in to
7. Except
9. into

CHAPTER 9

Exercise A

1. C
3. C
5. C
7. 2 (Calcutta; however,)
9. 2 (is, however,)
11. b
13. a
15. a

Exercise B

1. Compound
3. Simple
5. Compound
7. Compound
9. Simple

Exercise C

1. 1 (confidential,)
3. 1 (decision,)
5. 1 (invented,)
7. 0
9. 0

Exercise D

Answers may vary.

1. 2 (experience; however,)
3. 2 (faced, nevertheless,)
5. 1 (averages;)
7. 2 (month; in the meantime,)
9. 2 (employees, moreover,)

Exercise E

Answers will vary.

1. Bankruptcy can be either declared by the debtor or requested by the creditors.
3. Banks use computers not only to sort checks but also to disburse cash automatically.

5. Because old computer hardware creates hazardous dump sites, computer manufacturers are starting recycling programs. *OR:* Old computer hardware creates hazardous dump sites; therefore, manufacturers are starting recycling programs.

CHAPTER 10

Exercise A

1. D		11. 2 (Gamble, soap,)	
3. P		13. 2 (program, assistants,)	
5. I		15. 0	
7. D		17. 1 (possible,)	
9. D		19. 0	

Exercise B

1. D you prepare	7. P
3. I offices are located	9. I CPA disbursed
5. D he opened	

Exercise C

1. that	7. who
3. which	9. that
5. which	

Exercise D

1. 2 (Knight, Nike,)	11. 0
3. 1 (questions,)	13. 0
5. 1 (completed,)	15. 1 (decision,)
7. 0	17. 1 (space,)
9. 0	19. 0

Exercise E

1. a	7. b
3. b	9. a
5. d	

CHAPTER 11

Exercise A

1. date	Tuesday, September 11, 2001,
3. series	Alaska, South Dakota,
5. nonessential appositive	Darrow, lawyer,
7. independent clauses	considered,
9. terminal clause, afterthought	contract,
11. degree	Kivel, Ph.D.,
13. clarity (repeated words)	is,
15. adjacent numerals, date (comma optional)	2001, (or December, 2001,)
17. nonessential clause	Carp, Kodak,
19. short quotation	thing," Peters,

Exercise B

1. address   M. G. Warren, Drive, Miami, 30021,
3. parenthetical   people, of course,
5. C (short prepositional phrase)
7. direct address   you, Ms. Krause,
9. C
11. introductory verbal phrase   chair,
13. independent clauses   2003,
15. nonessential clause   Brightmail, protection,
17. clarity   long,
19. nonessential clause   Administration, 2003,

Exercise C

1. 4 (hope, Mark, Hannibal, Missouri,)
3. 2 (benefits, payroll,)
5. 4 (August 17, 1982, Monday, October 19,)
7. 1 (team,)
9. C
11. 1 (secondary responsibility,)
13. 1 (bookkeeper,)
15. 1 (231,)
17. C
19. 1 (meeting,)

Exercise D

1. independent clauses   rates,
3. independent adjectives   resourceful,
5. adjacent numerals   16,
7. abbreviations   Wille, Ph.D., Corloni, M.D.,
9. clarity   was,
11. clarity   unhappy,
13. introductory verbal phrase   keys,
15. numerals $2,000,000
17. prepositional phrase   year,
19. independent adjectives   overpaid,

CHAPTER 12

Exercise A

1. eBay;   7. C
3. Amazon.com;   9. said:
5. undertaking;

Exercise B

1. 1 (awards;)   7. 1 (Nation:)
3. 1 (rule:)   9. 1 (references;)
5. 1 (65 million;)

Exercise C

1. 1 (threat:)
3. 1 (international audiences;)
5. 1 (hackers;)
7. C

9. 1 (short passwords;)
11. 2 (review; that is,)
13. 1 (elements:)
15. 2 (monopoly, namely,)

CHAPTER 13

Exercise A

1. T
3. T
5. T

7. T
9. F

Exercise B

1. period
3. question mark
5. period

7. period
9. period

Exercise C

1. b
3. a
5. b

7. b
9. a

Exercise D

1. (2) (have you read it?)
3. (1)—Nelson Mandela
5. (2) managers (Courtney . . . Eastman)
7. (1) supervisor's
9. (2) (Detroit . . . Arbor)

Exercise E

Italics may be used instead of underlining.

1. (7) "In the arena of human life," said Aristotle, "the . . . action."
3. (4) "Capitalizing on Diversity" appeared in the book *Global Links*.
5. (4) said, "Our goal . . . restrictions."
7. (4) argument, his friend Kendra told him to "chill."
9. (4) titled "Nike Goes to Old School" in *Fortune?*
11. (1) Globex, Inc.
13. (3) manufacturers—Dell, IBM, and Hewlett-Packard—submitted bids.
15. (3) dates (February 15 and March 1) are suitable for the meeting.

Exercise F

1. (5) a.m. p.m. correspondence
3. (2) Dr. Medical.
5. (6) Tran, Schenk, c.o.d. shipment.
7. (3) Dr. 3 p.m.
9. (2) Dr. AFL-CIO.
11. (7) participants: Dr. Joyce Brothers, Mr. Dan Rather, and Ms. Barbara Walters.
13. (2) $45.95 account?
15. (6) U.K., U.S. taxes.

CHAPTER 14

Exercise A

1. a
3. b
5. a
7. b
9. a
11. a
13. a
15. b

Exercise B

1. (4) Marketing Research Department Far
3. (1) Director
5. (1) Fragile
7. (1) You
9. (4) Library of Congress African-American
11. (1) federal
13. (2) ex-Governor Governor-elect
15. (1) Midwest
17. (5) Big Mac french Coca-Cola
19. (2) northern winter
21. (3) state Supreme Court
23. (1) Yes
25. (10) Record Industry Association of America Those Those Those Internet United States

CHAPTER 15

Exercise A

1. a
3. b
5. b
7. b
9. a
11. b
13. a
15. b

Exercise B

1. 3489 Second Street
3. seven e-mail messages
5. 9 cents per issue
7. 9 p.m.
9. One Hampton Square
11. five departments with 14 computers and 16 desks
13. loan period of 60 days
15. Account No. 362486012
17. about 300 requests
19. C

Exercise C

1. 3, 4, 8
3. 16
5. No. 1245679
7. C
9. page 22, Volume 2, delete "dollars"

11. 50
13. 2 years, 6 months, $1.6 million
15. 21.5 million
17. (925) 685-1230 (or 925-685-1230 or 925.685.1230)
19. 18th of March, three

CHAPTER 16

Exercise A

1. *Due to* or *Because of* instead of *Due in large part to*
3. *about* instead of *in the neighborhood of*
5. *consider* instead of *give consideration to*
7. *for* instead of *in the amount of*
9. *Until* instead of *Until such time as*

Exercise B

1.	c	7.	a
3.	b	9.	c
5.	b		

APPENDIX C
ANSWERS TO UNIT REVIEWS

ANSWERS TO UNIT REVIEWS

UNIT 1 REVIEW—Chapters 1–3

1. a	26. a
2. a	27. a
3. b	28. a
4. c	29. b
5. a	30. a
6. a	31. a
7. b	32. a
8. b	33. a
9. a	34. d
10. b	35. c
11. c	36. a
12. a	37. b
13. b	38. c
14. b	39. b
15. a	40. a
16. b	41. b
17. d	42. a
18. b	43. a
19. b	44. b
20. b	45. b
21. b	46. a
22. a	47. b
23. b	48. b
24. a	49. a
25. b	50. b

UNIT 2 REVIEW—Chapters 4–6

1. b	10. a
2. a	11. b
3. a	12. a
4. b	13. b
5. a	14. b
6. a	15. a
7. a	16. b
8. b	17. b
9. a	18. c

19. b
20. a
21. 1 (building,)
22. 0
23. 2 (Lisa, brief,)
24. 2 (Grace, midnight,)
25. 1 (midnight,)
26. b
27. a
28. b
29. b
30. b
31. a
32. b
33. a
34. b

35. a
36. a
37. a
38. b
39. a
40. b
41. a
42. a
43. b
44. b
45. b
46. a
47. a
48. b
49. b
50. b

UNIT 3 REVIEW—Chapters 7–10

1. b
2. b
3. b
4. a
5. c
6. b
7. b
8. a
9. a
10. b
11. 0
12. 1 (office,)
13. 0
14. 1 (résumé,)
15. 1 (session,)
16. a
17. b
18. b
19. b
20. a
21. 2 (success; consequently,)
22. 1 (résumé,)
23. 1 (Capone,)
24. 1 (reported,)
25. 2 (believes, however,)

26. a
27. b
28. a
29. b
30. b
31. a
32. a
33. b
34. b
35. a
36. 1 (impression,)
37. 1 (week,)
38. 0
39. 2 (increased; moreover,)
40. 1 (bodyguards,)
41. b
42. b
43. b
44. a
45. b
46. b
47. a
48. b
49. b
50. a

UNIT 4 REVIEW—Chapters 11–13

1. 3 ('60, Ms. Welch,)
2. 1 (staff,)
3. 2 (recruiting, hiring,)
4. C
5. 2 (feels, however,)

6. C
7. 1 (Thursday;)
8. 3 (employees: integrity, intelligence,)
9. 3 (Integrity, intelligence, and drive—)
10. 2 (Nome, Anchorage,)

11. b	31. c
12. a	32. a
13. a	33. c
14. b	34. b
15. a	35. a
16. a	36. b
17. a	37. a
18. b	38. c
19. c	39. b
20. c	40. c
21. c	41. b
22. a	42. a
23. b	43. b
24. b	44. a
25. b	45. b
26. c	46. b
27. b	47. c
28. a	48. b
29. c	49. b
30. b	50. a

UNIT 5 REVIEW—Chapters 14–16

1. b	26. a
2. b	27. a
3. b	28. b
4. a	29. b
5. b	30. a
6. a	31. b
7. b	32. b
8. a	33. a
9. b	34. b
10. b	35. b
11. a	36. c
12. b	37. a
13. b	38. b
14. a	39. a
15. a	40. b
16. b	41. b
17. b	42. a
18. a	43. a
19. a	44. b
20. b	45. c
21. a	46. b
22. a	47. b
23. b	48. b
24. b	49. a
25. b	50. b

INDEX